MAXIM LEO

RED LOVE

THE STORY OF AN
EAST GERMAN FAMILY

Translated from the German by
Shaun Whiteside

D0108183

PUSHKIN PRESS

LONDON

Pushkin Press
71–75 Shelton Street
London WC2H 9JQ

Original title: *Haltet euer Herz bereit.*
Eine ostdeutsche Familiengeschichte. By Maxim Leo

First published by Pushkin Press in 2013
This edition published in 2014

006

The translation of this work was supported by a grant from the Goethe-
Institut which is funded by the German Ministry of Foreign Affairs

ISBN 978 1 782270 42 3

Set in Monotype Baskerville by Tetragon, London
Printed and bound by CPI Group (UK) Ltd, Croydon, CR0 4YY

www.pushkinpress.com

Praise for *Red Love*

'He describes these "ordinary lies" and contradictions, and the way human beings have to negotiate their way through them, with great clarity, humour and truthfulness, for which the jury of the European Book Prize is delighted to honour *Red Love*. His personal memoir serves as an unofficial history of a country that no longer exists... He is a wry and unheroic witness to the distorting impact—sometimes frightening, sometimes merely absurd—that ideology has upon the daily life of the individual: citizens only allowed to dance in couples, journalists unable to mention car tyres or washing machines for reasons of state'

Julian Barnes

'A searching and sensitive chronicle of three generations making the journey from euphoric hope to disillusionment to despair... [Leo] tells his tale through personal histories, in a terse, often elliptical style, well served by the translator Shaun Whiteside, that imparts an appropriately fablelike, once-upon-a-time quality to the narrative'

New York Times

'[A] compassionate memoir... By unpicking the loyalties of both political and family life, Leo honours the complicated motivations of real people, resulting in a humane, enlightening history of a collapsed country and a lost home'

Guardian

'This witty family memoir… describes life in the German Democratic Republic, with all the confusion, dashed hopes and conflicting versions of history'

Eileen Battersby, *Irish Times*

'[*Red Love*] gives us extraordinary, intimate access to East Germany when the state was not just in the family apartment but locked within the minds and aspirations of all its citizens'

Sunday Telegraph, Books of the Year

'A serious, very moving book… a weave of narratives about five lives, connected by blood and marriage but divided by politics'

Neal Ascherson, *London Review of Books*

'An important and compelling book for many reasons, but perhaps more than anything it reminds us of the pull of family, however flawed it might be'

Susie Dent, *Spectator*

'A family narrative that is simultaneously gripping and meditative, an engaging and thought-provoking portrait of a disappeared world'

Natasha Tripney, *Observer*

'Compelling… [Leo] is terrific at elucidating the slow, incremental steps by which people come to lie to themselves… guile, guilt and disappointment drip from these pages and *Red Love* is all the more affecting for it'

Marina Benjamin, *New Statesman*

'Written without political rancour or historical revisionism… With truthful tenderness and wry humour, Maxim Leo looks back not in anger but in an effort to understand the past'

Iain Finlayson, *The Times*

'In a wry, laconic style, [Leo] uses childhood memories to demonstrate how absurd "grown-up" behaviour can be – and how easily absurdity can morph into tragedy'

Maggie Fergusson, *The Economist*, 'Intelligent Life'

'Beautiful and supremely touching... Leo's memoir was the winner of the European Book Prize, and deservedly so... It is a moving saga of people who love one another but are doomed never to get along, and it is also an unbearably poignant description of a world that no longer exists'

Keith Lowe, *Sunday Telegraph*

'Tender, acute and utterly absorbing... With wonderful insight Leo shows how the human need to believe and to belong to a cause greater than ourselves can inspire a person to acts of heroism, but can then ossify into loyalty to a cause that long ago betrayed its people'

Anna Funder, author of *Stasiland*

'Honest and sober... a convincing depiction of what everyday life was like and the legacy it has left... illuminating'

Metro

'An absorbing and personal account that gives outsiders an insight into life in the GDR'

Shortlist

———————————

MAXIM LEO was born in 1970 in East Berlin. He studied Political Science at the Free University in Berlin and at the Institut d'Etudes Politiques de Paris. He has been an Editor at the *Berliner Zeitung* since 1997. In 2002 he won the German-French Journalism Prize, and in 2006 the Theodor Wolff Prize. He lives in Berlin.

CONTENTS

PROLOGUE

WHEN I STEPPED INTO the hospital room, Gerhard laughed. He said something. Weird, throaty words came out of his mouth. Then he laughed again. I can't remember my grandfather ever being so pleased to see me. The doctor told me the stroke had damaged the language centre in Gerhard's brain. All he could do now was express emotions. The rational side of him was blocked. I reflected that it had been precisely the other way around before.

Gerhard talked away at me. I pretended I understood. Eventually I told him that unfortunately I didn't understand anything at all. Gerhard nodded sadly. Perhaps he'd hoped I might be able to free him from his speechlessness. Just as I'd sometimes helped him out of his emotional stiffness in the past. With a joke or a cheeky remark that shook his authority. I was the clown of the family, the one nobody suspected of evil intentions. I could overstep the mark with the hero of the family, the man no one else dared to contradict.

A clear spring light shone through the window of the hospital room. Gerhard's face was slack and empty. We said nothing. I would have liked to have a conversation with him. I mean a real conversation. Usually conversations with Gerhard turned into monologues about his latest successes after ten minutes at the most. He talked about books he happened to be writing, about lectures he'd given, about newspaper articles people had written about him. A few times I tried to learn more about him. More than the stories everybody knew. But he didn't want to. Perhaps he was scared of getting too close to himself. That he'd got used to being a monument.

It was too late now. This man, for whom language had always been the most important thing, has become speechless. I can't ask him questions any more. No one can. He's going to keep his secrets.

Gerhard was a hero even before he entered adulthood. At the age of seventeen he'd fought with the French Resistance, was tortured by the SS and freed by partisans. After the war he came back to Germany as a victor and built up the GDR, that state in which everything was to be better. He became an important journalist, a part of the new power. They needed people like him at the time. People who had done everything right in the war, people you could refer to if you wanted to explain why this anti-fascist state had to exist. They sent him to schools and universities. Again and again he talked about his fight against Hitler, about torture, about victory.

I grew up with those stories. I was proud to belong to this family, to this grandfather. I knew Gerhard had had a pistol at some point, and that he knew how to use explosives. When I visited my grandparents in Friedrichshagen, there was apple cake and fruit salad. Again and again I asked Gerhard to talk about the past. Gerhard talked about frightening Nazis and courageous partisans. Sometimes he jumped up and acted out a play with different parts. When Gerhard played a Nazi, he pulled his face into a grimace and spoke in a deep, gurgling voice. After the performance he would usually give me a bar of Milka chocolate. Even today I think of those monster Nazis every time I eat Milka chocolate.

In the presence of adults, Gerhard wasn't as funny. He didn't like anyone in the family to "go around politicking", as he put it. In fact everybody who didn't, like Gerhard, believe in the GDR, was politicking around the place in one way or another. The worst was Wolf, my father, who wasn't even a member of the Party, but had married Gerhard's favourite daughter Anne, my mother. There were lots of arguments, mostly about things I only really understood later on. About the state, about society, about the cause, whatever it happened to be. Our family was like a miniature GDR. It was here that the struggles took place, the ones that couldn't be fought out anywhere else. Here ideology collided with life. That struggle raged for whole years. It was the reason my father went around the house shouting, why my mother secretly cried in the kitchen, why Gerhard became a stranger to me.

Gerhard and I sat together for a while on that spring day in that hospital room, which smelt of canteen food and disinfectant. It was slowly getting dark outside. Gerhard had caved in on himself. His body was there, but he seemed to be somewhere else. It may sound strange, but I had the feeling that the GDR only really came to an end at that moment. Eighteen years after the fall of the Wall the stern hero had disappeared. Before me there sat a helpless, lovable man. A grandfather. When I left we hugged, which I don't think we'd ever done before. I walked down the long hospital corridor and felt at once sad and elated.

That day I wished for the first time that I could go back to the GDR. To understand what had actually happened there. To my grandfather, to my parents, to me. What had driven us apart? What was so important that it had turned us into strangers, even today?

The GDR has been dead for ages, but it's still quite alive in my family. Like a ghost that can't find peace. Eventually, when it was all over, nothing more was said about those old struggles. Perhaps we hoped things would sort themselves out, that the new age would heal the old wounds.

But it wouldn't leave me be. I went to archives, I rummaged in cupboards and boxes, I found old photographs and letters, a long-forgotten diary, secret files. I asked my family questions, one after the other, for days, weeks. I asked questions that I'd normally never have dared go near. I was allowed to do that, because I was a genealogist now. And all of a sudden our little GDR was there again, as if it had been waiting to emerge again, to show off from every angle, correct a few things and perhaps lose some of the rage and grief that were still there.

On that journey into the past I became reacquainted with Gerhard, Anne and Wolf. And I discovered Werner, my other grandfather, whom I'd barely known until then. I think something was set in motion after that day with Gerhard in the hospital. A speechless man made us speak.

I

The Shop

I'M THE BOURGEOIS IN OUR FAMILY. That's chiefly because my parents were never bourgeois. When I was ten, my father walked round with his hair alternately dyed green or blue, and a leather jacket he'd painted himself. He barked when he saw little children or beautiful women in the street. My mother liked to wear a Soviet pilot's cap and a coat that my father had sprayed with black ink. They both always looked as if they'd just stepped off the stage of some theatre or other, and were only paying a brief visit to real life. My mates thought my parents were great, and thought I was a lucky person. But I thought they were embarrassing, and just wished that one day they could be as normal as all the other parents I knew. Ideally like Sven's parents. Sven was my best friend. His father was bald with a little pot belly, Sven was allowed to call him Papa and wash the car with him at the weekend. My father wasn't called Papa, he was called Wolf. I was to call my mother Anne, even though her name was really Annette. Our car, a grey Trabant, was washed only rarely, because Wolf thought there was no point washing a grey car. And he'd painted black and yellow circles on the wings so that you could see us coming from a long way off. Some people thought the car belonged to a blind person.

Sven's parents had a colour television, a three-piece suite and cupboards along the wall. In our house there were only bookshelves and a seating area that Wolf had cobbled together from some pieces of baroque bedroom furniture. It was quite hard on the bottom, because Wolf said you didn't need to be comfortable if you had something to say. Once I drew a plan of our flat the way I'd have liked to have it. A flat with a three-piece suite, a colour television and cupboards along the wall. Wolf laughed at me when he saw it, because the policeman's family that had lived there before had furnished it exactly as it was on my plan. He told me it was stupid and sometimes even dangerous always to do what everybody did, because it meant that you yourself didn't have to live at all. I don't know if I understood what he meant at the time.

At any rate, from the beginning I had no other choice but to become a sensible, orderly person. At the age of fourteen I ironed my shirts, at seventeen I wore a jacket and tried to speak proper German. It was the only way I had of rebelling against my parents. It's their fault that I became a good, well-dressed revolutionary. At twenty-four I got my first job, at twenty-eight I was married, at thirty the first child came along. At thirty-two a flat of my own. I'm a man who had to grow up early.

When I stand on my balcony and bend over the railing, I can see the shop where I was born. The shop is only two houses away, on the right down on the corner. You might say that I haven't moved much in my life. Thirty yards in thirty-eight years. I have no memory of the shop, we moved away when I was a year old. Wolf says they often put me in the street in my pram because the air in the shop was so damp. The shop was Wolf's first flat of his own. 26 Lippehner Strasse, Prenzlauer Berg, Berlin. His studio was in the front, towards the courtyard at the back there was a dark connecting room and a

Anne, Wolf and Maxim in Basdorf, Summer 1971

little kitchen. The winter of 1969, when Wolf and Anne met, must have been quite a hard one. The snow was three feet high in the street, and the tooth mug was full of ice in the morning. The first time Anne came to visit, Wolf had heated the stove in the bedroom and put a coffee bean on the bedcovers, like in a hotel. Because the rest of the flat was cold, they ended up in bed pretty quickly. Two months later Anne was pregnant. She always says I was an accident. And the way she says it, it sounds more like Chernobyl than a happy chance. Maybe they wanted a bit more time on their own, just the two of them.

Today there's an engineering office in the shop. Whenever I walk past, a grey-haired man is sitting motionlessly at his desk. You can just see his head and his feet, because the big shop window has a broad strip of frosted glass in the middle. Sometimes I think the man is a dummy. An engineer who stops at the waist. Perhaps that's why I've never dared to ask if I could take a look at the shop.

The house next door used to be a butcher's shop. The butcher lady used to slip my father packets of bacon pieces, because she knew he didn't have money for things like that. An aristocratic lawyer from southern Germany who bought the house a few years ago sometimes plays saxophone in the empty room, still tiled as it was in the old days.

Diagonally opposite was a soap shop whose lady manager recorded exactly which women went in and out of Wolf's house and sometimes confronted him about it. Today it's a design office, run by an American with an asymmetrical fringe, who listens to nothing but opera.

In the photographs that Wolf took of the street in those days, you see grey, broken walls and kerbstones with no parked cars. Wolf's scooter stands outside the shop. Everything looks empty, forlorn. Today the street is a dream in pastel colours. Gold leaf gleams from stucco facades, and it's hard to find a parking space. The people who live in the flats are couples in their late thirties who feel more as if they're in their late twenties. They are men with expensive sunglasses and women who wear tracksuit jackets with short skirts. They push buggies with sports tyres, buy their meat at the organic butcher's and emanate that feeling of complete effortlessness that always implies a lot of effort. I live here, and to be quite honest I fit in pretty well.

That's what Wolf thinks too. He sometimes laughs at me for needing so many things to be happy. Because I'm one of the others now. The Westerners. He can't believe what's happened to his son and his street. I wonder about that too. I don't know how it happened, how the Easterner in me disappeared. How I became a Westerner. It must have been a creeping process, like with one of those highly infectious tropical diseases that spread undetected in your body for years, and eventually take control. The new age has changed my street, and me too. I didn't need to move, the West came to me. It conquered me in my own home, in my familiar surroundings. It made it easy for me to start a new life. I have a wife from France and two children who don't even know that there was ever a Wall in Berlin. I have a well-paid job on a newspaper, and my chief concern at the moment is whether we should have floorboards or a stone floor in our kitchen. I don't need to take a position on anything, I don't need to be committed, I don't need a point of view. Politics can be a topic of conversation if you can't think of anything else. Society isn't the main subject of my life, I am. My happiness, my job, my projects, my dreams.

That sounds so normal, and perhaps it is. Nonetheless, I sometimes have a bad conscience and feel like a turncoat. Like someone who's betrayed his past. As if I were still a bit guilty for my first life, as if it were forbidden to leave the things from those days alone. Now, that life in the GDR strikes me as strange and unreal. It's as if I'm reporting from a distant time that has hardly anything to do with me. I feel like one of those old men who sit in a pink television studio telling Guido Knopp about the siege of Stalingrad. I've become an eyewitness, a man who experienced something a long time ago. Like my grandfather, like all the others who were someone else in their youth.

But in fact the East isn't far away at all. It clings to me, it goes with me everywhere. It's like a big family that you can't shake off, that people are always asking you about, that's forever calling you up. Even in my little family, the East is always there. I sense him when I visit Wolf, who's now living a few streets away, in an attic that was once his studio. He moved there after he split up with Anne five years ago, when bourgeois coupledom became too constricting for him. Apart from his study area there's a bed, a circular dining table, two chairs, a home-made shower and a toilet separated off by a curtain. Wolf says it's enough for him. He's opposed to all that luxury, consumerism, dependence on money and status. He wants to live modestly and be free, as he had been right at the start in his little shop. Anything else would actually have been difficult, because he didn't earn that much money after the Wall came down, and only gets 600 euros' pension a month. Financially speaking, he says, things in the GDR were much more straightforward than now because things like the flat and food were almost free, and only luxuries really cost any money. Again and again we urged him to prepare for his old age. But Wolf refused to worry about the future. "I hope I'll be dead by the time

Anne and Maxim, 1970

I'm sixty, I don't want to rot away in some old people's home," he said. Now he's sixty-six and fit as a fiddle.

I don't find it easy to be with Wolf in his attic, so I usually invite him to ours. Compared to his poverty, our affluence looks completely ridiculous. I have this constant nagging feeling that I should be justifying myself. I probably find it harder than he does, because Wolf is really content with very little. He has quite a young girlfriend now, and all the time in the world. He says he hasn't felt so great in ages.

Wolf had lots of time in the GDR as well, or at least that's how it always seemed to me. He made good money, and was able to work just for a few months a year. The rest of the time he made art. And took holidays. We had a little house with a big garden in Basdorf, in the north of Berlin. We spent our two-month summer holidays there, and usually our one-month winter holidays as well. My little brother Moritz, Wolf and Anne and me. We went on cycling, canoeing and skiing trips. Today the whole of my childhood seems like an endless holiday. Wolf was good at football, climbing trees, building huts and high-diving. So I wanted to be a bit like him. As free and strong as that.

Anne's a lot calmer and more sensible than Wolf. She doesn't take herself so seriously, either, probably a good start if you want to live with a man who thinks he's the centre of the world. When I think back to my childhood, I see a woman in front of me, sitting in the corner with a book and a glass of tea, emanating such deep calm and contentment that you'd have to feel pretty important to risk dragging her from her absorption. Anne says she didn't really know what to do with me at first. She was twenty-two when I was born, and in the photographs from those days she looks like a fragile princess who shouldn't be exposed to too much reality. There's a photograph of her holding me in her arms. Her pretty, pale face is turned slightly away from me, and her dark eyes gaze longingly into the distance. It was only when I started to read that she really started getting interested in me. I got the books that she'd been keen on when she was a child, and she was delighted if I was as keen on reading them as she had been.

When she first gets to know Wolf, Anne's impressed by his rough, rebellious manner. He's so entirely different from the men she's met before. He's cheeky, he's an artist, he breaks the rules that she always respects. And he's a handsome man with merry eyes and a goatee that gives him a slightly raffish appearance. The first time they go out together, they walk through the snowy park that starts at the end of my street. The paths are slippery, and Anne is wearing the wrong shoes, as always. Wolf takes her by the hand and leads her through the park, and somehow she knows she's found a protector. Someone who won't let go of her again.

They talk about politics, about the country they live in. Wolf tells her how terrible he finds this GDR, how uncomfortable he feels, how much he hates having these old men speaking on his behalf. Anne says she's in the Party. Then Wolf stops, lets go of her hand and falls silent. "Everything couldn't have been right all at once," he said later. It's the start of a long love and a long argument. With my parents, the two things always went together.

Anne talks about her father Gerhard, the Communist who fought the Nazis in France. She paints the picture of a tender hero who loves his Party and his daughter. Wolf talks about his father Werner, the little Nazi who became a little Stalinist. A man he doesn't know much about, a man he fell out with. Wolf says he wished he could find a new father back then. He likes the tender hero Anne tells him about.

Before Wolf is invited to Anne's parents for the first time, they ask Anne if the new boyfriend is in the Party as well. When Anne says he isn't, her father's face darkens, and her mother advises her not to take it too seriously each time she falls in love. Wolf says today that it was all quite clear already, before he even saw her parents. Anne says that's overstating the case.

At any rate she's got a birthday, and there's a dinner at her parents' place in Friedrichshagen. Anne barely slept the night before, because she'd been summoned for a Socialist auxiliary unit on the railway, along with some other students. A set of frozen points had to be cleared of snow. But in fact all they did was stand around, because there weren't enough shovels. Anne thinks it's stupid that she has to join units like that as a student. Gerhard is annoyed. He says: "If there's a problem in Socialism, everyone has to help." His voice is unusually harsh. Anne doesn't understand why he reacts like that. They defend themselves, one word generates another. Wolf looks on in silence and wonders whether this is really the man Anne has said so many good things about. Eventually Gerhard says, looking at Anne, "When it comes to the crunch, you're on the other side of the barricade."

I heard that sentence often later on, mostly from Wolf, who quoted it time and again as proof that it was Gerhard's fault if the family never really came together. When we were doing the French Revolution in school, my history book had a picture of a barricade in the streets of Paris. I imagined my parents on one side and my grandparents on the other. I didn't know which side I was supposed to be on. I just wanted everyone to make sure we were a real family. Without a barricade.

Anne grabs her clothes, takes a fat blanket and moves into Wolf's shop-apartment. For a while her mother tries to talk her out of her new love. She says Wolf is a wayward artist, not someone you can depend on. And he isn't intelligent enough for her, either. It's only when her parents discover that Anne's pregnant that they give up the fight. The marriage takes place at Prenzlauer Berg register office. In the wedding photograph Anne wears a short floral dress, her belly swelling slightly beneath it. She has her hair up and looks like a girl. Wolf wears a dark suit and grins into the camera. Gerhard stands beside him wearing a serious expression.

The wedding is celebrated at Anne's parents' summer house. A French friend of the family grills marinated meat, there are roasted snails, baguettes, olives and claret. The guests speak French and English, they wear expensive suits and make jokes about the GDR. Wolf is impressed by the party. He's never been to a barbecue before. He doesn't know you can eat snails. He sees his first pepper mill, takes out the peppercorns and then doesn't know what to do with them. The others laugh, he blushes. Anne introduces him to her parents' friends, writers or journalists who lived in exile in France, America, Mexico or Shanghai during the Nazi era. Wolf listens to their stories about fighting, fleeing and suffering. They are people unlike any he's ever met before. Heroes, survivors from the big wide world who have found their new home in the little GDR. Because they aren't persecuted here, because they are safe here. Their stories are so different from those of his family. It's all so strange. Wolf wonders if he can ever belong among these people, this family, this woman he's just married. Gerhard raises a glass to him without looking at him. They drink to a happy marriage and a long life.

2

Secrets

I ALWAYS THOUGHT IT WAS brilliant that Anne came from the West. It gave her something special, and it gave me something special too. As a child, I sometimes cleared out her handbag and looked at all its contents. On her ID card it said: born on 25.2.1947 in Düsseldorf. Anne explained that the city was in the Rhineland and quite rich. I knew Aunt Hannah and Uncle Paul lived in Düsseldorf. They drove a white Ford estate car, and once gave us a Carrera Bahn, a Scalextric set, which I still think was great of them. I never understood how Anne could have been so silly as to move to the East. I knew there were people who went to the West. But I'd never heard of anyone doing it the other way around. Anne said I should be glad because I wouldn't even have existed if she'd stayed in Düsseldorf. That sounded logical enough.

While she's still living in Düsseldorf, Anne sometimes stands at the window with her great-grandmother Bertha, watching the people in the street. Bertha divides the passers-by into orderly and disorderly. You can tell the disorderly ones because they swing their arms when they walk.

Anne's family live in a huge, grand apartment on Jürgensplatz, which was assigned to Gerhard when he got back from France. As

Gerhard and Nora, 1948

recognition of his combat in the French Resistance, Gerhard had been promoted to lieutenant in the French Army, and in Germany an officer of the victorious forces has a right to a suitable apartment. The people who had lived in the flat before were a Nazi family who had been interned by the British. Anne's parents took over the furniture, because they didn't have anything themselves. It must have been strange living with the enemy's furniture, but they probably had other concerns at the time. There are photographs of Anne as a child, lying on a brown bearskin. Gerhard calls the skin "our Aryan bear". He is working as a journalist with the Communist newspaper *Freiheit*, where Anne's mother is also employed as a secretary. At the weekend Anne goes to the swimming pool with Gerhard. She throws a comb into the water and he brings it back like a trained seal. In the evening before they go to bed Gerhard sings old partisan songs or plays the accordion. He can tell stories and and draw pictures for them at the same time. As far as Anne's concerned he's the most brilliant father in the whole world.

One day Gerhard is gone. Anne's mother says he had to go and work in another city and will be back soon. Time without Gerhard is boring, because her mother can't play the accordion and doesn't much feel like telling stories. A few weeks later, in February 1952, Anne and her mother go on a skiing holiday in Oberhof in the Thuringian Forest. They stay in the "Ernst Thälmann" Party holiday home and wait for Gerhard, who turns up a few days later. They celebrate Anne's fourth birthday together. The same evening there's a conversation between the parents. Gerhard says they're not going to go back to Düsseldorf because there's a danger that he might be arrested there. From now on they will live in East Berlin, the comrades had already got everything ready. Anne's mother asks no questions. She's used to there being things she'd rather not know. A driver takes the family to Berlin in a black Wolga. They drive to a house in Pregelstrasse in Prenzlauer Berg. There's a flat there that's already been fully furnished, and a few things have already arrived from Düsseldorf. They are given passports with new names. They are now called Oswald. Two comrades tell them it's very important to forget their old names as quickly as possible. A few months later, Anne's grandmother visits from Düsseldorf. She tells Anne it's entirely normal to get a new name when you move to a new town. Anne thinks that's perfectly reasonable.

In the family, the explanation for the hasty move to Berlin was always that Gerhard was persecuted as a Communist in the West, and therefore preferred to help build up the GDR rather than be pushed around by reactionaries. I only discovered the true reason for the flight to the East after the GDR had already collapsed. When my father's secrets could no longer be kept.

In Berlin there's a playground in front of the house, and lots of children who meet in the afternoon and move around the area without their parents. For Anne this is all new and exciting, and she's soon forgotten Düsseldorf. In the neighbourhood there's a Pioneer troop where they do crafts and sing. Her parents tell her that they now live in a country where everyone's free and equal, where the good people are in charge and where her Papi doesn't have to be frightened any more. Two years later they move to Friedrichshagen and all of a sudden they're called Leo again. Her parents say she mustn't tell anyone that they were once called Oswald, so that the bad people can't find them. Anne has a favourite children's book, *Oswald the Monkey*, that she no longer dares to read. In Friedrichshagen her parents tell their new neighbours that they've come straight from Düsseldorf. On one occasion the owner of the house meets Anne on the stairs and asks how come she's got such a strong Berlin accent. Anne freezes with fear and says, "That's how they talk in Düsseldorf as well."

Two years later Anne takes the train to Düsseldorf with her mother and two sisters. It's their last visit to their family in the West. On the border at Helmstedt the compartment door is pulled open and a fat man in uniform asks to see their papers. He flicks through a black book and asks Anne's mother her husband's first name. To Anne's great amazement, her mother refuses to give out any information at all. The man becomes angry and asks again and again. Eventually his eye drifts towards Anne. She is sliding uneasily back and forth on her seat, her lips pressed together. She's worried that she might divulge her father's secret name if she opened her mouth even slightly. The seconds under the quizzical eye of the uniformed man seem long and unbearable. In the end the West German border guard furiously closes the compartment door and goes.

All these secrets, the worry that the bad people might come and get her beloved father after all, must have left a deep mark on Anne. Long before she can understand what's happening around her, the Cold War has slipped into her little world and made her a comrade. For Anne the world is divided into two camps from the outset. There are the good people, including her father most of all, and there are the others, the ones you fear and fight against. As her father did, as her father's friends did, as everyone who feels a spark of decency must do. For a long time Anne thinks the GDR is full of such courageous fighters, until she understands that she and her parents belong to a tiny minority. To a minority that took power in the GDR, and who nonetheless feel strange in this Germany from which they were once banished.

In Friedrichshagen there's a tall, white-haired man in the neighbourhood who has an English hunting dog which the children are sometimes allowed to stroke. Anne is even allowed to take the dog out on a lead. The old man has serious conversations with her, and once he invites Anne to his house. Anne must have been ten or eleven at the time, and she feels very flattered. There is hot chocolate and biscuits, and all of a sudden the man starts talking about a night when lots of houses in Berlin were on fire. The man is very worked up, and tells her how sorry he was "that your department stores were on fire". Anne is baffled, she doesn't know what the man is talking about. His hands wave in the air, copying the flight of the burning bales of material. Anne imagines she can see the fire of that night blazing in his eyes. She contradicts him, saying that her parents never owned any department stores. Ah, the man replies, of course you all had department stores. He also talks about a girl who lived in his house and looked very like Anne. He says he was so sorry that she "went away".

27

Anne goes home rather confused, and tells her parents about her strange encounter. They get worked up too and explain that the man was talking about Kristallnacht. "Because we're Jews, he obviously thinks we owned department stores as well," Gerhard says. Anne doesn't know what it means to be a Jew. She just knows that Gerhard had to leave Germany when he was still a child. She feels a strange anxiety, a sense of helplessness, of strangeness.

Downstairs in their building live the Holzmanns, who her parents say are Jews. Herr Holzmann had been in Auschwitz, and had lost his family there. Later he had married again and had a son called Benjamin, the same age as Anne. One day the Holzmanns ring the doorbell, bringing matzos. They wish the family good health and a happy Pesach. Anne's parents are visibly unhappy about this visit, which Anne doesn't understand because the Holzmanns are nice people and even brought something nice to eat. Anne asks what Pesach is, and her mother tells her that's the name the Jews give to their Easter festival. It's clear that they themselves don't want to be Jews.

Gerhard once told me he fought as a Communist in the war, and not as a Jew. I think being Jewish for him means not being able to defend yourself, being a victim. He once told me how he fled the advancing German troops in July 1942 in France, and hid for a while in a Jewish children's home based in a castle near Limoges. One day French police came to the home and wanted to take all the children away. Gerhard had locked himself in a room in a tower and watched from above as the children were hunted. Some of them tried to escape, but were caught by the police, loaded onto trucks and taken to Drancy internment camp. When Gerhard told me about this experience, he was much moved. Perhaps it was then that he made his decision not to be caught as easily as that, but to fight for his convictions. He found it honourable to die as a Communist, but being chased as a Jew struck him as possibly undignified.

As a child Anne knows hardly anything about what her family suffered during the Nazi years because they were Jews. She doesn't know the experiences of her mother, who only escaped deportation in the Rhineland by the skin of her teeth. She knows her grandfather died in Auschwitz, but has no idea why. She only gradually discovered her father's story. He only ever tells her the adventurous anecdotes from which he emerged victorious. How they blew up the tracks on which the German reinforcements were due to arrive, how they sat around the campfire and sang dirty songs, how he shot an SS man who had been chasing him in a forest. She's glad her father is such a jolly hero. Most of the other heroes she hears about at school are serious, old men. Gerhard keeps the sad and painful stories to himself. Once Anne comes into the bathroom just as he's brushing his teeth. She notices that Gerhard has no incisors in his upper jaw. When she asks him about it, he quickly puts in his bridge, laughs and asks what teeth he has missing. Then Anne knows she's asked a forbidden question, and that there are things he'd rather not talk about.

Most of all, Anne really wants to be like all the other children. But it's not as easy as that. Again and again she comes up against the realization that she's different. Because she's the only one in her class who doesn't take part in religious-studies classes, because no one else has a father who gives political lectures at school, because from the start she's been the group leader of her Pioneer organization. Anne is so filled with the feeling of representing the right cause that she even corrects the teacher when one of his statements doesn't seem quite partisan enough. Some of her fellow pupils avoid her, she's the "Red", the eager one.

When Anne is thirteen, she moves with her parents to Geneva. Gerhard has been appointed UN correspondent with the East German news agency ADN, and because the comrades in Berlin think it's unsuitable for East German children to attend a Swiss school, Anne is taught at home by her mother. Anne learns French in the street, and later, when she goes to the Soviet Embassy school, Russian as well. At the weekend they go to the mountains or swim in Lake Geneva. For Anne it's an exciting, carefree time. The only strange thing is that the people in the West aren't nearly as bad as she'd thought. The working class aren't exploited, either, they're rich. The janitor who sometimes fixes things in their flat drives a bigger car than her father.

After a year Anne has to go back to the GDR because the Soviet Embassy school only goes up to year seven. Her parents and two younger sisters stay in Geneva. In fact Anne is supposed to go to a home for East German diplomats' children, but her parents think it's better to leave her in Friedrichshagen, in a familiar environment. Frau Schenk, an old woman from the neighbourhood, moves into her parents' flat and takes care of Anne. Now life isn't as exciting as it was, and Anne often feels lonely, but she accepts it all because it's the only way. Only today does she wonder how her parents managed to leave her on her own for two years just because the Party had decided that East German children can't go to a Western school.

The best thing about this time is the holidays, because she's allowed to fly to Geneva on her own. She sits right at the front in the first row on the plane, and the stewardesses stuff her full of Swissair chocolate. Once she has to change in Prague. The GDR ambassador to Czechoslovakia, a friend of her father's, collected her from the gangway and helped her pass the time in the transit lounge. On one flight she sits next to a young Cuban, with whom she immediately falls in love.

When the Wall is built in August 1961, Anne is in Geneva on her summer holidays, and isn't really aware of it. Her parents think it's a good thing that there's a proper border now. A protecting rampart to keep the bad people out of the country. It's only when she comes home after the holidays that Anne notices what's happened. Her fellow pupils, who aren't allowed to go to the West any more, confront her in the classroom, demanding to know why she of all people should still be allowed to travel. It's a kind of tribunal. She feels the hostility of the others, their rage. One of them shouts that the GDR is a prison, a lousy dictatorship in which only Red officials thrive. She stands alone in front of the furious crowd, supposed to defend something that she herself barely understands. She is the fourteen-year-old ambassador for a state that is busy saving its own skin.

When she comes home to the big empty flat, she walks around the table in the dining room over and over again, mumbling aloud the arguments that didn't occur to her in class. It's as if she has to reassure herself of her own attitude. She has no one she can talk to about it all, no one with whom she can share her insecurity and unease. Her parents are far away. Every week she sends at least one letter to Geneva, but she doesn't write about that experience. Perhaps she doesn't want to worry her parents.

I found Anne's letters from those days in a cupboard at my grandparents' flat. In neat, girlish handwriting she records all the important things that are happening in Berlin. Once, visiting her friend Monika Scharf, she sees a film on television telling the story of the resistance fighter Werner Seelenbinder. Anne writes: "In the afternoon they showed the film *One of Us* on television. Herr Scharf must have been annoyed that his children got a chance to see the truth. For example there was one scene in which Communists were beaten down by Nazis. Then Herr Scharf said: 'Well, they're exaggerating very nicely. This film is just a load of rubbish, because it wasn't like that.' And Frau Scharf said, 'Now they're turning everything around in the film, and people still believe it.' Then the Hitler Youth marched onto the screen. Then Herr Scharf said, 'That's just like the Pioneers.' But I said, 'In the old days children had to join the Hitler Youth, and with the Pioneers it's voluntary. And Pioneers are brought up for peace, the Hitler Youth weren't.' On Monday I looked at a few of Monika's books. There was one book that was called the *Young Girls' Book*. I came across one sentence: 'The Young Girls' Association is part of the National Socialist Movement.' Then I said to Monika, 'Hey, let's cover up the words National Socialist so that no one can see them.' And we did."

It's as if, at the age of fourteen, she already feels responsible for a state, for the historical truth. In another letter she writes, "I argue so much with Monika about political matters. I'm sure you've heard that the Yanks are trying to provoke people at the border, and whole units have already crossed the border and then went back. And an East German policeman was run over. We talked about that at school, and I asked Monika what she thought about it. She said she'd seen it on television and the Yanks only marched up to the border and the policeman hadn't been run over. It turned out that she'd been watching Western television, and that's not allowed."

Two weeks later she writes to say that the Holzmanns, the Jewish family from their block, had escaped to the West. "This morning, just before I went to school, there was a knock on our door. I opened up, and standing outside were two men from a removals firm who wanted to collect something from the Holzmanns. They asked us if the Holzmanns were there, and Aunt Schenk said, 'The boy's already gone to school, and if no one opens the door, it means there's no one there.' Then, when the men had gone, she said to me, 'I'm sure Frau Holzmann is still there. She just doesn't open up when she hasn't got dressed yet.' When I came home from school, the door was bolted, because the Holzmanns are in the West now." That the two men from the removals firm were actually from the Stasi and that Aunt Scheck might have made it easier for the Holzmanns to escape by telling a little lie, my mother didn't know at the time. But she was very preoccupied with the subject of West-East flight. In a letter just before Christmas she reports that a classmate fled with his whole family. At the end of the letter she writes: "I don't know why they would do that."

3

Convictions

W HEN ANNE IS SEVENTEEN, she is sent by the school to a District Committee event organized by the SED, the Socialist Unity Party. They sit together in a big hall, are served ham sandwiches and coffee and listen to lectures by important comrades. Even the head of the Berlin SED is there. He says the city's best and most mature students are gathered together that day because some serious and important issues need to be discussed. The mood is solemn, as if they are about to be initiated into the most confidential Party matters. Anne feels a certain pride rising up in her at the thought that she of all people is allowed to be here, among the best. She learns that the GDR faces big and important tasks that can only be mastered if young people actively help. The time of spectating is over, the Party head says, now something needs to be done for the country and for peace. The Party head pauses, looks right and left and says at last, in a muted voice, that the precondition for this is to become a member of the SED. When she hears this, Anne can't help laughing out loud. A few students look at her in bafflement, and even she is shocked by her own reaction. But this attempted recruitment drive strikes her as so crass that all the pride she felt a moment before flees in a trice. Just now she would have been willing to do anything for peace and the country. Now she consoles herself with the fact that she is, after all, only seventeen, and only adults are accepted into the Party.

After the lectures they are all supposed to write a poem on the subject "I must make a decision". This is followed by individual discussions. Suddenly Anne is sitting opposite five comrades who ask her if she could imagine becoming a candidate for the SED, the Socialist Unity Party of Germany. Anne says she can imagine that very easily, but as she is only seventeen she will have to postpone that decision by a year. One of the comrades looks at her seriously and says they might make an exception in her case. There's the possibility of applying for special authorization from the Party Central Committee. Anne feels her heart beating faster, she's excited about this possibility. Special authorization from the Central Committee! She imagines how amazed her father will be, how amazed everyone will be. She signs immediately, leaves the room in a state of elation, has a sense of having experienced something great. At the end, the Party head from Berlin speaks again. In his speech he quotes from the poem that Anne wrote. She sits there blushing to her roots, it's like a dream. On the way home she looks at her reflection in the shop windows. She feels so different, and thinks that people must somehow be able to see that too. She tells herself that from now on she'll never again suffer from lovesickness or any other silly problems. Because she will soon be a comrade.

For Anne, the Party is more than an organization, more than the people gathered together in it. The Party is like a supernatural being, something terribly big and remote from normal life. When Anne hears her parents talking about the Party, she senses their respect, faith and devotion. When he talks about the Party, her father's voice assumes a particular tone. He speaks more quietly, cautiously, articulately, as if the Party might somehow be listening, and might rebuke him for a false thought, for a slip of the tongue. The Party is absolute truth, absolute wisdom, which is why only enemies of the Party would even think of criticizing it or imagining they're cleverer than it is. Individual Party members might fail, might make mistakes. The Party never makes mistakes. This belief in the great Whole, in the "cause", as they call it at home, is her comfort later on, when she sometimes despairs of banal everyday life in the GDR. Anne says she was prepared to put her life at the service the Party in those days, to be absorbed into it.

When Anne talks to me about these things today, she sometimes starts crying. Perhaps out of rage, because she was so naive, but perhaps also out of disappointment that it didn't work. That this state and this Party, which cost her so much energy, simply disappeared like that. I think my mother's relationship with that state was like an unhappy teenage infatuation. She had fallen for the GDR as a young girl, and it took her a lifetime to break free of it again. It's hard for me to understand all this, to see that my cool, intelligent mother is still grieving for that first great love even twenty years after the end of the GDR. How deeply embedded inside her it must still be, that hope, that unconditional desire to be there when it came to freeing the world from evil. I myself wasn't really aware of her faith. That may have something to do with the fact that it was no longer strong enough when I reached the age at which politics started to become important. But it could also be that she deliberately spared me from it because she knew how hard it is to resist your parents' convictions.

It's strange interviewing your own mother. Seeing her fighting back the tears. Anne sat in her study, in the armchair that used to have a brown and yellow pattern and is now covered with a grey woollen fabric. She wanted to say something, but her voice broke, immersed in the feelings that cling to her memories. Normally I wouldn't have probed, I'd have left her alone. Children get used to being cautious, to reining in their curiosity. Children don't want to see their mothers crying. I had to remind myself not to be a child, but a genealogist interviewing one of his major characters. I couldn't give her a hug, however much I might have wanted to. Anne took deep breaths, wiped away her tears. I saw the little wrinkles around her mouth, the grey hair which she only dyes a little bit because she doesn't want to look like her mother, who has had raven-black hair for forty years. That afternoon, Anne seemed older to me than she usually does. That might be partly because we were talking about her youth. I have those photographs in my head, her girlish face, her big, dark eyes. It struck me that, to me, Anne has actually always stayed the same age. A timeless woman. "OK, let's go on," Anne said, and resumed her story.

She wants to be a journalist. She knows the profession from her father's work, and she think it's great that you can be paid for being curious. As far as she's concerned, journalists are people who know an incredible amount and can also write brilliantly. Her model is Egon Erwin Kisch, the famous reporter who was always in search of the truth and usually found it.

In 1966 she starts work as an intern on the *Berliner Zeitung*, at the age of nineteen. And again she's something special, because everyone knows her father, who is admired not just as a resistance fighter but also as a journalist. That doesn't make things particularly pleasant for her, because no one really takes her seriously. She's only ever the daughter. But much worse is her disappointment with the way the newspaper works.

On her second working day she takes part in a meeting in which the editor-in-chief explains what's not to be written about right now. The meeting is called an "argumentation assembly", and it always takes place when the editor-in-chief has just been to see the Central Committee, and been informed of the latest prohibitions and censorship measures. It isn't just a matter of how to place and understand certain events in Party terms. They are also told what words are henceforth undesirable because the enemy has appropriated them, what products can't be mentioned because they're defective. There are months in which no one is allowed to write "washing machine" or "car tyre". "Social Democracy" is expunged for two years, "parliament" and "the Angolan People's Front" only for six weeks.

Lists are drawn up, with daily updates of what may be written and what not. But if someone writes a wrong sentence, uses a suspect turn of phrase or an unusual word, there is a meeting in which the colleague in question has to explain himself. At which remorse is required. Once an elderly editor from the local section writes that soot is produced when lignite is burnt. This essentially harmless statement is severely castigated by the editor-in-chief, because it might be read as a criticism of air pollution from lignite stoves in the GDR. Again and again it is dinned into the journalists that the enemy never sleeps, and the censorship department in the Central Committee certainly doesn't.

At first Anne works in the political section. Most of the articles printed here are Party press releases supplied by the ADN news agency and just have to be pasted in. None of the press releases can be shortened or altered in any other way. Even spelling mistakes are left as they are, because no one dares to phone the Central Committee about something like that. Anne notices that most of the bosses aren't really journalists at all, but Party officials doing their duty on the paper. The good journalists aren't in the Party, which she finds strange, because the Party is, after all, supposed to be the elite. Because there is hardly any room for independently written articles, most of them have hardly anything to do. They start drinking in the office at midday. The bosses drink most of all. The journalists try to do the dirty on each other. There are plots, denunciations, smear campaigns. And a paper is produced along the way.

Anne is shocked by this state of affairs. She tells her father, who is currently running the foreign-politics section of the central Party organ *Neues Deutschland*. She asks if things like that happen on his paper as well. As always when he finds a particular topic disagreeable, Gerhard doesn't reply. And as always, Anne doesn't press him. A friend of her father's explains to her that that's how it is almost everywhere in the East German press. "Where people lie, they also have to drink," he says and smiles sadly.

On the evening of 8 May 1968, Anne puts her first lie in the paper. She's on the late shift, and is sitting at a long table in the news department. The telex machine is ticking away next to her. The department manager hands her a sheet of light-blue paper of the kind usually used for the official communications of government offices. But the sender's name is missing from this particular piece of paper, and it isn't clear where the report comes from. The department manager says she should quickly stick the page onto manuscript paper and take it to the typesetters. Anne sticks the story on, reads it quickly through and gives a start. The headline is: *American Tanks in Prague*.

According to the short piece, observers had seen American tanks in the streets of Prague. Anne knows about the things that are currently happening in Czechoslovakia, about the reform movement that will later be called the "Prague Spring". She knows the official line. The East German papers are writing that anti-Socialist forces are at work, trying to remove the power of the people under cover of reform. She herself isn't entirely sure what to make of events in Prague, or whether it's really as dangerous as people claim. But she knows that this report can't actually be true. If the American Army really had invaded Prague, it would have been massive news, it wouldn't have been a small story on page two. She goes to the department manager and asks what the article is supposed to be. "Don't ask," he says, "write it up and send it down." Anne insists that there must be something wrong with the story. But the boss waves her away. "Send it to the typesetters, that's all that concerns you." She's gloomy and uncertain, but she does as she's told.

The next day letters of protest and angry phone calls come flooding in. Even the Czech Embassy complains. The editor-in-chief passes the calls on to Anne. She, the intern, is supposed to explain to these furious people something that cannot be explained. She doesn't dare distance herself from the report. When it's over, she feels miserable. She still doesn't understand what's actually happened or what's going on. Two days later there's another report. This one says that filming is currently under way in Prague for a film about the city's liberation from fascist occupiers. The American tanks seen in the streets were part of the historical setting. It's only much later that Anne understands the purpose of the strange reports. She understands that they were intended to spread uncertainty, to suggest danger, to provoke. She understands that she was, that evening, a small cog in a big propaganda machine. Today Anne says she should really have bidden farewell to her dream job right then, because she could have realized that journalism in the GDR was impossible without a lie. But she hadn't got there yet.

These stories of my mother's seem ghostly to me. I can't imagine how she could spend two years working on that paper without losing her faith in goodness. Thirty years later I myself started work as an editor on the *Berliner Zeitung*. It was my first real job as a journalist. By then the newspaper belonged to a big Hamburg publisher, and everything was exactly as Anne had dreamt it would be. Because now you could actually write what you wanted. Because now it really was all about knowing something and getting the most exciting stories possible into the paper. There were colleagues my mother's age who had been on the paper for thirty years, and who had had to go through the same things as she did. I would have loved to know how they dealt with the lies, how they coped with suddenly being free journalists. But I didn't dare to ask, I would have felt like a self-appointed judge asking questions for which there may not be any answers.

In August 1968 Soviet tanks roll through Prague, and this time it isn't a film that's being made, it's reality. Anne is working as a child-carer in the *Berliner Zeitung*'s company holiday camp. The camp director calls a meeting and passes on the official declaration that the Czech government has called upon the Soviet Army for help. Anne believes this version, and only learns the true course of events from West German radio a few days later. That the government of the ČSSR had been ousted in a Soviet military coup. That the head of government, Alexander Dubček, and his ministers had been arrested. That the reform movement had simply been defeated. On Western television, Anne sees the pictures of bloody demonstrators in Prague, bravely defying the tanks. She hears about people being killed, injured, taken prisoner. During those days something inside her dies, something that she can't yet quite name. She feels betrayed, cheated. Not only by GDR propaganda but also, much worse, by the GDR's big brother in Moscow, whom she had seen as a just and peace-loving ally. In the editorial office in Berlin she reads *L'Humanité*, the French Communist newspaper. She learns that the comrades in France are protesting against the invasion, and she is a bit relieved, because you can clearly be opposed to the invasion even as a Communist.

Anne also learns that friends of hers in Berlin have been arrested for distributing flyers against the invasion. These are Thomas Brasch, with whom she went to school, and Bettina Wegner, whom she has known for ages. Both come from similar families to her own, she's often sat down with both of them and talked about Communism and the GDR. She knows that neither of them are enemies. And she wonders if she herself would have helped to distribute the flyers. If she had been in Berlin, if they'd asked her. She's pretty sure she would have joined in. Not because she's particularly brave, but because she wouldn't have believed that anybody could be locked up for something like that. She thought things like that happened to other people, people on the side of the bad people. Now she doesn't feel quite as sure as before, when she was convinced that nothing could actually happen to somebody like her. She understands that when it comes down to it the state doesn't differentiate.

Thomas Brasch and Bettina Wegner will later go to the West. Brash will become a well-known poet, Bettina Wegner a celebrated singer. But for now both of them are in prison in the GDR. Because they wrote on a few pieces of paper in felt-tip pen. "Hands off Red Prague" and "A Dubček for the GDR", it said on the pieces of paper that Thomas Brasch put through letter boxes at night in Prenzlauer Berg. His own father denounced him to the police in the end. Horst Brasch, like Anne's father, comes from a Jewish family, and he too emigrated to the West during the Nazi era. It's the same story, the same conflict, except with dramatic consequences. Anne talks to her parents about the arrests. Gerhard says the invasion was necessary for the cause. If anyone doesn't understand that, they aren't part of it. Anne says, then she isn't part of it, because she too would have been willing to distribute flyers. Her parents look at her in horror, as if she is a lost child. They never mention the subject again.

4

Accusations

A NNE WANTS TO STUDY HISTORY. She thinks it's a good subject for a journalist. She wants to specialize, and once she's a
specialist in a particular area, she'll be able to write about it in the
paper and no one will be able to contradict her, because specialization
is the most important thing, she thinks. She's already repressed her
experiences on the *Berliner Zeitung* to some extent. She tells herself
you should always be wary of generalizations.

In September 1968 she begins her studies at the Humboldt
University in Berlin. In the first week her seminar group is summoned to sign a declaration in favour of the Soviet Army's invasion
of Czechoslovakia. It's a test of their sympathies. Anne sits in a little
room with the other students. They hardly know each other, none of
them knows how far they can go, how the group will react. Most of
them seem rather clueless. The subject has been discussed for weeks,
many people in the country are opposed to the invasion, but only a
few dare to say so openly. Anne's thoughts are tumbling around in her
head. Only a little while ago she had claimed she would be prepared
to distribute flyers against the invasion, and now she's supposed to
sign this declaration. Everything within her resists, she doesn't want
to give in just like that, betray herself. On the other hand she'll have

terrible problems if she refuses. She'll be thrown out of university, she may never study again. It would all be over before it had even started. She feels that this day might bring a life decision. Anyone who gives in once will do it over and over again, and anyone who has been punished will never wash that stain away.

Anne suggests rephrasing the declaration. It said in the paper that the arrested Czech reformers had delivered a declaration along with the Soviet government in which they agreed to continue the reform process along Socialist lines. At that point Anne doesn't yet know that the agreement amounts to a capitulation by the reformers. Anne writes that the seminar group emphatically supports the Moscow declaration. The passage about agreement with the invasion is deleted because it's no longer about the past, it's about the future. Everyone signs with relief. They haven't agreed, and neither have they resisted. They have managed a small diplomatic feat that spares their careers and their conscience. But for Anne it's still a defeat because she wasn't brave, just cunning.

At the first Party conference at the university the lecturers ask Anne if she wants to become Party secretary for the first-years. The lecturers don't know her, but they've read her political files. In them, under origin, it says: "progressive intelligence". That's the premium category, a kind of Communist mark of nobility. Her "Parteibürgen"—more or less her Party godparents—are listed as Rudi Goguel, a famous and highly respected comrade, composer of the famous "Moorsoldaten" song and her father's best friend. Harald Hauser, a former French Resistance fighter and prominent author, and Ursel Herzberg, who lived in exile as a Jew in London and later became a state prosecutor. These first-class references are tickets into the young Party elite. In her final reference from the *Berliner Zeitung* it says: "Overall Annette should be seen as a cadre with the capacity for further development, who has the intelligence to grow into a useful cadre in our society if properly directed." In plain language: here is somebody who has very respectable gifts but must still be trained under strict supervision.

The first Party assembly at the university is a dreadful spectacle. Two lecturers are told to stand at the front by the board. A comrade rises to his feet and declares that the two of them aren't worthy members of the SED because they have attacked the Party and the working class with their hostile speeches. Their reactionary, revisionist behaviour discredits the whole university. A comrade whispers to Anne, telling her what's going on. The two lecturers clearly dared to express doubts about the correctness of the Soviet invasion of Czechoslovakia. They hadn't actually protested against the invasion, but just asked whether this action by Moscow was reconcilable with the peaceful partnership of the community of Socialist states. Now one comrade after another gets to his feet and hurls criticism and contempt at the two men. They stand there, heads lowered, as if petrified, and don't dare say anything themselves. They look like rabbits acting dead so that the snake won't eat them straight away.

Later, Anne often returns to that scene. In her imagination the two men are wearing pointed hats and signs around their necks with self-denunciations written on them. Anne finds this assembly so frightening that she undertakes to be even more careful from now on. She understands that conditions at the university are very different from those in the newspaper office where she'd been working. On the newspaper, no one demanded that you believe in what you do. It just needed to work. Here in the university even the purity of thought is checked. Anyone who doesn't declare unconditional loyalty is isolated. Later she sometimes sees the two punished lecturers in the student canteen. They are always alone, no one dares to talk to them or even to join them. They still keep their heads lowered, they are penitents in perpetuity, a warning to the others.

I asked Anne if she felt guilty because she'd played along. She nodded mutely, stared past me, clung to the arms of the chair as if she would fall to the ground if she wasn't careful. It was silent in her study and after a few long seconds Anne said she had somehow held such considerations at arm's length. It had preoccupied and depressed her, but at the same time she had sensed that she had to protect herself against too much sympathy, because she couldn't have borne it otherwise. She was twenty-one, she wanted to study and have fun, she still believed in the great Whole, even though she had quiet doubts.

Anne makes friends with a few students who are already in their third year. They are intelligent, witty lads who seem much braver than she herself feels. These lads want to develop a new form of FDJ (Free German Youth) work. Not as ideological, more transparent, more open. They invite Anne to join in. There are to be regular meetings in a flat. Anne finds the offer weird, she senses danger. A month later the third-year FDJ group is dissolved, and the lads are suspended from university. One of them has to work in a power station for two years, and is only allowed to continue his studies after that. Another is luckier. Because his father is head of a department at the Academy of Sciences, he is allowed back after a year. Anne talks to one of the excluded students. He says he hadn't expected that they would respond so harshly to these harmless discussions. He says he wouldn't do it again, it was a mistake. This witty boy is now a broken man.

The professor in charge of Anne's seminar group tells the students to condemn the suspended men. A declaration is prepared, speaking of hostile individuals who want to pervert the spirit of the FDJ. This time Anne speaks out, because she knows very well that the accusations are false. She gets up and says she knows these students, they aren't enemies at all, so it would be a mistake to condemn them. The professor is surprised to hear these words from the Party secretary. She throws him. All of a sudden other students who are also opposed to a condemnation speak out as well. One says that not all criticism needs to be deemed hostile, because then no one would dare to say anything at all. The professor explains that the suspended students had collected signatures against the demolition of the Garrison Church in Potsdam. "As students of history you will know, of course, that Hitler signed a pact with the clergy in that church. Anyone opposed to the demolition of that church is making common cause with Fascism."

No one knows what to say to that, not even Anne. She does sense that the professor's argument is perfidious, because it assumes certain things that none of the punished students had even thought of. On the other hand, of course there's nothing worse than being suspected of making common cause with fascists. Only later did she work out that for the Party ideologists Fascism is always the last argument if nothing else works. Her father did the same thing if he didn't know where to take an argument, if the madness he was defending became too mad. "I risked my life for that," was the sentence that silenced Anne at home. It was a killer argument which drew a line that she didn't dare to cross.

I too remember a citizenship lesson in which the teacher explained to us that the song 'Special Train to Pankow' by Udo Lindenberg was forbidden in the GDR because it was fascist. The teacher quoted part of the lyrics in which Udo Lindenberg accused our General Secretary, Erich Honecker, of sometimes wearing a leather jacket and listening to West German radio in the toilet. "This is a clear reference to the leather jackets of the Gestapo, and Lindenberg is thus defaming a man who spent years in prison under National Socialism. We don't want to hear this Nazi song." Even at the time I knew that this account was complete nonsense. But I didn't dare to say anything. Because "Nazi song" sounds so dangerous.

Anne's experiences at university make her cautious, but not silent. On 11 December 1968 she reads an article in the newspaper *Junge Welt* that infuriates her. It is about the songwriter Wolf Biermann, who was violently attacked by the media in the GDR because he said negative things about East Germany at concerts in the West. The article quotes sentences from poems by Biermann, to prove the indefensible hostility of his attitudes towards the GDR. Anne sends a letter to the editor. She writes: "You are reviewing poems that no one knows. You back up your criticism with scraps from his poems. That is inadmissible, because the next line of the poem might say the opposite. You want young people to accept your opinion without resistance, and without having any independent thoughts of their own (after all, they can't read the poems you are attacking for themselves). I don't think this makes any sense for us. I think you are right to criticize his attitude. But you are achieving precisely the opposite with your article, which is full of clichéd and unfounded expressions. You are driving our young people onto Biermann's side, as most of them are opposed to Party slogans and won't believe you."

I think this letter gives a very good account of Anne's attitude at this time. She doesn't criticize the fact that a songwriter isn't allowed to express his opinion in the GDR. She accepts that, because she too thinks Biermann's opinion is dangerous. On the other hand, she also thinks it's intolerable that someone like Biermann should be countered in this way. She writes: "You engage in diatribes against Biermann that do not correspond to your superior and commanding position. You write about 'his big mouth'. Do you need to do that? I don't think it's good to abuse someone with expressions such as this." In the end she is essentially true to the core of the matter, and only has reservations about the form. Because enemies are also human. A few decades later Anne finds that letter in her Stasi file. She learns that an operational procedure had been launched against her. But the case is dropped a short time later. "Father of the woman in question is a member of the Central Committee of the SED," it says in the file. And this is an end to the matter, because investigations aren't usually carried out into important Party workers and their families. Where would Anne's life have gone if she hadn't had her father to protect her?

I'm surprised that the Stasi wasn't clever enough to recognize my mother's loyalty. Others would later be mistaken about her as well. That may be because she was a very unusual case. A fiery fighter for Socialism, who said heretical things. The daughter of a prominent Party member who allowed herself her own opinion out of the security of her faith. Which was in the Party, but also in truth. She thought the two things actually belonged together. Anne says she was always rather alone in her political attitudes. She wasn't faithful enough for the faithful, too uncritical for the critical. She wanted to belong somewhere, but it didn't work.

Wolf says he sometimes almost despaired at her naivety, her unshakeable convictions. He sees how much she suffers from her faith, how she struggles with it. When the West German Chancellor Willy Brandt comes to Erfurt in March 1970, they both sit in front of the television. On East German television you see the Chairman of the GDR Council of Ministers, Willi Stoph, and the people of Erfurt shouting, "Willi, Willi". On West German television you see that the people only start shouting when Brandt steps to the window. This outright lie by GDR propaganda makes Anne furious. She sits there and can't do anything but cry. Wolf says obviously they lie in the East. She mutely shakes her head.

Anne and Wolf's first real argument is about whether people who escape across the GDR border are traitors and should be punished. Anne thinks the border must be defended, and if people who don't respect the border aren't punished, then you might as well knock it back down again. During this conversation Wolf stays quite calm by his standards, even though he can't quite believe what she's saying. Maybe it's just that he's horrified. He thinks you can't actually live with a woman like that, but at the same time he has the feeling that not living with her would be just as impossible. He remembers standing with his friend Manfred by the border checkpoint at Teltow, aged nineteen, at the end of August 1961, two weeks after the building of the Wall, and wondering whether he should leave or not. The barbed-wire fence was two and a half metres high, it isn't even a proper fence yet, strictly speaking it's just five wires half a metre apart. You would just have needed to lift the wire in the middle a bit and you'd have been through. Tall weeds grow behind the fence, and the next border post is a long way away. There isn't actually

Anne, 1970

a risk, just the fear of doing something wrong, leaving his mother alone, interrupting his training as a retoucher. But it could also be that these were nothing but excuses, that he didn't actually know what he wanted. That he lacked courage. And it was all so clear. He knew the GDR, he must have known what to expect if he stayed. Most of his friends had left already. Why did he hesitate? Later Wolf often wondered whether it had been the biggest mistake of his life. He doesn't even know to this day.

After Wolf and his friend Manfred have been standing by the fence for half an hour, lost in thought, two border soldiers come by and arrest them. They are questioned, have to spend the night in a barracks cell and are then released again. Perhaps the guards believed that they didn't want to escape, that they were just daydreaming. Wolf says he didn't believe at the time that the border would really last. A month later he is called up to the National People's Army. He is among the first year of recruits, one of the first men to take up arms in the service of the GDR. Now he is in, and won't be getting out again.

When the Wall went up, Wolf was nineteen years old, the same age as I was when the Wall came down. It's possible that he had just as little understanding of the historical significance of the moment as I did when I stood by Checkpoint Charlie in Berlin on 9 November 1989. The first thing I thought of when I stepped onto the soil of West Berlin was that I'd left my cigarettes at home. I was really annoyed about that, because I always smoke when I'm excited. I had no Western money to buy cigarettes, and I didn't dare ask anyone for one. I thought about what the Westerners would think of me if I started begging as soon as I'd taken three steps into freedom. I wondered if I should quickly go back to the East, fetch my cigarettes and come back later. But I wasn't sure they'd let me out a second time. And it struck me that I didn't really know if they'd even let me back in again. If a Western reporter had asked me at that moment what I felt at the time, I'd probably have said that this Wall coming down was really stressful. And I didn't spend that much time in the

West because I had to go to work very early the next day. Even today I'm embarrassed that I turned up at exactly seven o'clock in my lab at the Academy of Sciences on 10 November 1989, where the only other person was a colleague who hadn't seen the news.

5

Street Children

I WAS SITTING WITH WOLF in his attic room, at the circular dining table. It was quiet, only the occasional noise from outside drifted in through the open window. Wolf seemed to be agitated. He slid back and forth on his chair, trying to find a beginning. A beginning for his life, which he was now going to relate. He spoke slowly and with great concentration; sometimes he closed his eyes for a moment, tracked down his memories, became the boy who ran through the ruins in Freienwalder Strasse with his mates. Like Anne, Wolf was born in the West. In Berlin-Gesundbrunnen. He talked about streets overgrown with grass and weeds, of the smell of lovage filling the air. American soldiers played football with their steel helmets, and in the untended allotments there was a Gypsy camp with an old fortune-teller, who read your future in your palm for twenty pfennigs. Grandma Sigrid, Wolf's mother, had her fortune told there. Apparently there had been an argument about payment, and the fortune-teller put the evil eye on Grandma Sigrid and told her that her husband was going to leave her. Unfortunately a few years later the old Gypsy was proved right, which is why even today Grandma Sigrid can't stand anyone who looks remotely like a Gypsy.

*

For the children, the city is one enormous adventure playground. Even at the age of six Wolf moves around the area with his pals from dawn till dusk. They are a gang, and gangs stick together. They climb on piles of rubble, make dens in abandoned basements and balance on joists sticking out of the ruins. They catch ladybirds, put them in shoeboxes and run all over the city trying to find leaves for their ladybirds. The city is busy, the streets are full of people. War-wounded sit on the pavements playing music, locksmiths, carpenters, dairymen work in backyards.

Sometimes they head out to Marzahn, where unexploded ammunition is stored in a dump. They start fires, throw in machine-gun straps and run for cover. The noises of the flying bullets are so terrifying that some of them shit themselves with fear. The bigger boys break the detonators off the flak grenades and pour the black powder into bags. They go into ruins with intact chimneys. The explosive goes into the oven door, the fuses are shoelaces dipped in weed-killer. They light them and run like hell. And when the charge goes up behind them and the huge chimney falls to the ground like a toppled giant, they shout and dance with joy. The grown-ups never ask where they've been. They have their own life.

They only come home when they're hungry, and for the first few years the hunger never goes away. Wolf's mother Sigrid makes soup from turnip stalks, and Wolf and his little sister Rita nearly throw up when the stalks get stuck in their throats. They have a room and a kitchen, the toilet is half a flight of steps down. The room is damp and the tiled stove is usually cold, because there's been no fuel in Berlin for ages. Most of the trees have been cut down, and the big, fat trees that no one dares fell have no lower branches. When the wind blows cold Wolf has to sit by the window and wait for a branch to fall from the crown of the tree. And if one does come down, other boys go after it too.

Every two weeks Sigrid goes foraging in Vehlefanz near Oranienburg. She digs in the fields for turnips and potatoes. Sigrid also always brings a big bundle of kindling with her, carrying it around on her back for hours on end, for fear that someone might steal it before she gets home. Werner, Sigrid's husband, is still in France as a prisoner of war at this point. She has to bring up the children on her own. She sells the toys, the breakfast boards, the coffee cups to get hold of a bit of bread and margarine. Sometimes at night she weeps quietly to herself over life's injustices.

In the middle of October 1947 a telegram arrives from Werner. He writes that he's just been released from imprisonment, and that he will be home soon, probably around the eighteenth. Suddenly Sigrid starts whistling tunes when she gets up in the morning. She tells the children their Dad is coming home soon. Wolf is delighted, and at the same time he realizes that he doesn't know what his father actually looks like, or how his voice sounds. When Werner went off to war in November 1944, Wolf was two years old. He has no memory of him, nothing. Wolf knows only that everything is going to be fine. His mother said so.

Sigrid buys flour and a few eggs on the black market. It takes up a good share of her monthly allowance, but she doesn't care because she is absolutely determined to bake a cake for her husband's home-coming. Days before he is due to arrive, they scrub the flat, wash the laundry. Sigrid irons the good tablecloth, a neighbour cuts the children's hair. The evening before he is due to arrive, Sigrid puts a bunch of flowers and the cake on the tablecloth. Wolf is so excited that he can't get to sleep. He thinks he'll probably never have to worry about anything ever again once his Dad is home.

At eight o'clock in the morning Wolf hears voices from the kitchen. And then there he is, that tall, strange man. He strokes Wolf's head, he has brought a piece of chocolate, and basically everything's just as Wolf imagined. But after only a short time he realizes that Werner isn't going to sort everything out after all. He's irritable and terribly tired. Any confusion, any noise, any problem, however small, makes him lose his temper completely. He shouts, quivers with fury, then sits apathetically on his chair again for hours on end. Werner escaped death as a Wehrmacht NCO at the Front, was imprisoned in camps, where he saw his comrades die in their hundreds. He spent over a year toiling on a farm in western France. It took him weeks to get back to Berlin. To his family, to his old life, the one he dreamt of in prison, which gave him the strength to survive. And now at last he's there—and he's finished.

Werner remains a stranger to Wolf for a long time. Sigrid had told him about an athletic, handsome, funny man. Someone who can do everything. The Werner that Wolf meets is gaunt, restless, nervous. One day after he comes back, Werner goes out to collect twigs so that they have fuel for the oven. A week later he registers at the labour exchange. He looks like someone who's afraid of waking up. He gets up at six o'clock in the morning and dusts the room. His urge for order and cleanliness is frightening. The children get on his nerves. One evening when Wolf is whining because he doesn't want to go to bed, Werner thrashes the living daylights out of him. The next morning Wolf can't sit down, his bottom is covered with bruises. Werner goes on to beat him often, hitting him so hard that Wolf flies across the room. Sigrid doesn't dare stop her husband. She thinks that's how it has to be, she puts up with it. They're glad when Werner isn't there, when peace returns. Wolf says that over time Werner was at home more and more rarely. The family takes breakfast together. As a returning soldier, Werner gets an extra ration of butter and eggs. He carefully peels the eggs, cuts them into slices and eats them all himself. The children eat thin milk soup and watch.

Once Wolf is caught smashing the windows of a factory with his friends. The factory owner demands that the windows be paid for. Werner sits down at the table with Wolf and calculates what the damage will cost the family purse. In the end Werner says Wolf has to go, because there isn't enough money left for everybody. Sigrid packs a little rucksack, they say goodbye, and then Wolf walks off, convinced that from now on he'll have to get by on his own. He sees his parents standing by the door and doesn't even cry. He thinks that's just how things are. At the next street corner Werner catches up with his son and tells him that the lesson was intended to teach Wolf the seriousness of his crime. He is allowed back home.

I wonder if Werner understood what a terrible moral his pedagogical exercise left behind. How shocking it is for a six-year-old child to think that he might be banished from home by his father for a stupid prank. Werner probably expected Wolf to burst into tears and plead for forgiveness. But Wolf wasn't like that. A few months later Werner does the same thing all over again. He locks Wolf in the basement because he can't bear it when the siblings argue. Instead of complaining, Wolf wraps himself up in a bicycle cover and goes to sleep in the basement. It is a struggle between the two of them.

Werner becomes a teaching assistant in a vocational school in the Russian-occupied zone. It's just by chance that a job happens to be available there. His wages are paid in Ostmarks, which is a problem, because they live in the West, where money from the East isn't worth much. Once a week the children go shopping for food in the East with their mother. They drag the heavy bags back across the Bornholm Bridge into the West. Wolf hates that bridge because it's so long. When he has to go and get milk on his own, he always pauses in the middle of the bridge. He spits on the empty railway tracks and imagines he's an engine driver, powering a big, black steam locomotive through the city. It would be a very special train that didn't need tracks, one on which you could bring the heavy milk jugs right up to the front door. In November 1949, they move to Schönhauser Allee in the East. It's a practical decision, not a political one. At the time no one could have predicted that the different sectors were eventually to become different countries.

When schoolchildren are chosen to be sent to the countryside, Wolf is usually among them. He's thinner and weaker than the others in his class. Once they are sent to Glowe on the Baltic coast. In the morning there's a flag parade and five jam sandwiches. For lunch there's soup with cod liver oil. They stay in a former prisoner-of-war camp. There are huge sheds and barbed wire on the perimeter fence. Wolf thinks the camp is weird. He wants to put on weight as quickly as possible so that he doesn't have to come here again.

At home Werner starts talking about Socialism, which will soon sweep all poverty away. Werner is now studying at the College of Education in the newly founded GDR, and is excited about the idea of a new society. He absorbs it all like a thirsty man, like someone who urgently needs something he can believe in again. Once Werner comes home from his training and explains that even the Socialist family needs new rules. From now on the children are to say not Papa and Mutti, but Werner and Sigrid. And they're to swim naked in the lake, and the children are to join the Pioneers.

In the evening, Sigrid has to go with Werner to lectures on the origins of Communism. She doesn't understand a word of what's said there, but she goes along so that Werner doesn't get cross. On the First of May the family demonstrates on Unter den Linden. A woman puts a carnation in the buttonhole of Wolf's jacket, Werner wears his dark suit and Sigrid a floral dress. They walk past the ruins, through the Tiergarten, where no trees stand. They sing songs about the united front of the working class, about the rise of the proletariat, who have finally lost their chains. Wolf wonders where the chains went. He has a book about a pirate captain who attacks ships and frees the enslaved oarsmen. The slaves wore chains too, and were glad to get rid of them. It seems to be a good thing.

In the summer of 1951 there is a World's Fair in Berlin. The young people of the world are invited to bombed-out, post-war Germany. Wolf drives through the city on a truck along with the other children. They sing songs, and in the evening they go to a stand and pinch food parcels, which include a piece of salami. Wolf has never had salami before. He takes it home, cuts it into thin slices and eats it all himself.

One weekend Wolf goes with Werner to an exhibition about the first Five-Year Plan of the GDR. At the way in there's a blue plastic badge with a Five on it for the children. Werner explains that in five years' time people in the GDR won't have money any more, because everyone in the shop will just take what he needs. Werner points to the plans and tables hanging on the exhibition walls. They are proof of the superiority of Socialism. Wolf can't imagine how that's supposed to work. But five years is a long time for a nine-year-old. It's possible that Socialism will get that far, who knows. And anyway, they now have so much to eat that no one needs to go hungry.

It's less fun in the Pioneers. There are constant appeals and processions. Agitators come and say things that nobody really understands. Wolf and his sister are the only ones on their street who wear the white shirt and the blue scarf. The other children tease them for it. In November 1951 Werner moves out of the house. He tells the children that he and Sigrid don't love each other any more, so from now on they're going to live apart. Sigrid stands by the ironing board and cries. Wolf is allowed to call her Mutti again, doesn't have to swim naked and doesn't have to go to the Pioneers. Because Werner took the sofa bed away, in the evening they set up a little camp of mattresses in the sitting room. Wolf lies next to his mother. As he falls asleep he feels her warmth, hears her breath. It's a lovely feeling.

6

Thugs

AFTER SCHOOL WOLF and his mates go to West Berlin, often smuggling themselves into the border cinemas to watch cowboy films, and steal chocolate and sweets. The West is gaudy and exciting. It smells of coffee and chewing gum. The American soldiers, who sometimes give them little presents, are as cool as the cowboys in the films. No comparison with the East German police who guard the border crossings in their ill-fitting uniforms. Every day they go back and forth, from one world into the other. They see the neon signs and the red banners, gleaming Daimler coupés and Russian military vehicles, women in sheer stockings and apron dresses. They listen to rock 'n 'roll and workers' songs. Wolf says every child knew at the time which the superior system was. The East strikes him as increasingly helpless, increasingly pitiful. On 17 June 1953 he takes the tram past Alexanderplatz. He sees the Russian tanks, hears the shots from Keibelstrasse, where the big prison stands. He goes home and thinks that the GDR might be over soon. In a few days the uprising has been defeated, and everything goes on as if nothing had happened.

Every other Sunday Wolf's mother dresses him and his sister up smartly, and then the children head off to Stalinallee. Werner lives there, on the first Socialist street of the Republic. They walk past the Stalin Monument, larger than life on its patch of green. Stalin wears a military jacket and the same severe expression as Werner when he's explaining something important. The way to Werner's flat passes through a huge stairwell covered with marble slabs. There is a lift and a refuse chute. It's a palace. But a palace in which workers and peasants now live, says Werner. He himself is a school head-master, but that's not important. What is important, says Werner, is that you feel like a worker. Wolf doesn't like these Sunday visits. It's like citizenship classes. Werner asks how things are going with the Pioneers, and they don't dare say that they stopped going ages ago. He reads to them from newspaper articles that he finds instructive. They are about production figures, about successful housing projects. He can't explain why there are no jeans in the East. Then he refers to the wider political situation, to the West, which is obstructing the young Republic whenever it can. When Werner speaks about the workers' paradise, Wolf thinks about the old women who stand outside the coal shop opposite their house every day, waiting for a few briquettes to fall off the truck. He thinks about the shops in West Berlin where there is a surplus of everything. The reality he knows and the things Werner tells him don't really match up.

Later Wolf stops going to Stalinallee. He can't bear those lectures any more. In a former air-raid shelter on Storkower Strasse he has set up a party room with other young people. They dance rock 'n 'roll and comb their hair back with soapy water. He practises his dance steps on the handle of the sitting-room door. He meets his first girls, there is snogging and also a bit of fumbling. On special occasions Wolf wears a red velvet jacket with gold buttons and tight, black trousers that mustn't be more than fifteen centimetres across the hem. Now he's a rocker, a thug, the kind of guy who won't be fobbed off with bullshit. When they dance openly at a fair in the Plänterwald, the police come. Dancing openly is forbidden in the GDR. Girls and boys are separated, pushed onto trucks and dropped in a forest near Oranienburg. They walk back to Berlin in the rain at night, humiliated, put in their place. A few months later they set up in an abandoned summer house in Blankenburg. They listen to Elvis and Bill Haley and dance in the dark until they drop. Here again, the police sometimes come by, confiscate their tapes, note their names and ID numbers. Wolf says they really just wanted to have some fun, but the stupid state always immediately did something political. Anyone who wears jeans and slip-on shoes is a class enemy. Anyone who stands on the street corner with a transistor radio is threatened by helpers of the People's Police. Listening to Western radio and forming groups is forbidden. If you comb your hair into a DA, you have to stand spread-eagled against the wall while your ID is checked. Wolf says it was eventually just about the principle. Whether you were for or against. "They were always showing you that you didn't belong. They turned you into the enemy."

Wolf assumed that role. He probably didn't see himself as an enemy, but more as someone who didn't go along with everything. That balance between conformity and resistance, between courage and betrayal, is hard to explain. Even those words are probably too big to describe the little movements that were generally at issue. It was a grey area of possibilities, in which you could go in one direction or another, in which there was no right way and no wrong one, but at best the feeling of having found a bearable compromise. Anyone living in that grey area had to keep reacting afresh, had to constantly reconsider everything. He wasn't a traitor or a hero, he could only try to be as true to himself as possible.

I think Wolf himself often didn't know why he did certain things and not others. For example there was that business with Walter

Ulbricht, the General Secretary of the SED, known to some as "pointy-beard". In the early Sixties, Wolf is working as an apprentice retoucher in the printing works of *Neues Deutschland*, the central organ of the SED. During the late shift a photograph of Ulbricht comes in, which needs to be prepared quickly for the current edition. Ulbricht wears rimless glasses that make his goatee beard look a little more modern. There's something wrong with the contrast of the photograph, and Wolf paints around the glasses—until all of a sudden Walter Ulbricht is wearing horn-rimmed spectacles. No one notices the change, the paper goes to print, and the next morning two men from the Stasi come to the printing works and want to speak to Wolf. They ask him who authorized him to mock the General Secretary, and Wolf says there was no authorization, if anything it was a mistake. One of the men says that people have gone to prison for mistakes like that. But in the end they believe him, and just give him a severe warning.

A few weeks later the new fast train line to Pankow is opened. The train no longer passes via Gesundbrunnen, my father's old home, because the Wall is there now. The new line is a symbol, a sign from the Socialist capital. There is a photograph of the first fast train coming into the station, decorated with flowers, and Wolf brushes out part of the train so that all that is seen is part of the engine, which looks rather strange. This time the Stasi aren't as nice, they question my father for hours, wanting to know who was behind it. He can't explain how this new error was made. He himself is quite baffled, because he doesn't know what actually possessed him. It's something between an accident and a provocation. The Stasi men see his bafflement, but they also see that he isn't an idiot. They shake their heads and say that the door to prison is now wide open. Hostile propaganda, the vilification of senior representatives of the state, it doesn't get much worse than that. But something keeps them from punishing him severely. Perhaps they see that he isn't actually an enemy, just someone who's seeing how far he can go. Or else they think he's interesting and they have other plans for him. This might explain the many attempts they will later make to recruit him. At any rate, Wolf is let off lightly. He is sent to Leipzig as a "Socialist assistant".

His banishment to the provinces is enjoyable at first. Wolf arrives in Leipzig in the autumn of 1962, just before his twentieth birthday. It's carnival time. He goes dancing almost every evening, and as a good-looking Berliner it isn't hard for him to meet people, making his stay a very pleasurable one. There's still a proper bourgeoisie in Leipzig. On Saturdays well-brought-up girls go to the tea dance at the Ring Café. Wolf wears pointed shoes with seven-centimetre heels, pinstripe trousers and tailored shirts. The women think he's great and exotic. He meets one who takes him home, to a villa near the racetrack. There's a black grand piano in the drawing room, and the girl's father invites Wolf into the library, where smoking is permitted, for a chat. After that Wolf spends almost every weekend at the house, there are musicians and cocktail parties. The family has its own box at the opera, to which Wolf also has access, and eventually he stops feeling as if he's in the GDR.

His work as a retoucher on the *Leipziger Volkszeitung* isn't particularly demanding, and as a "Socialist assistant" he earns more than he did in Berlin. He also manages to find himself some private commissions, so that he suddenly has plenty of money. He takes taxis rather than trams and eats in restaurants. Wolf has his dancing shoes made to measure, and soon his shirts and trousers too. He likes the city, likes its easy-going elegance. It's so unlike Berlin, where the bourgeoisie has either fled or gone into hiding, where the workers and officials from Saxony have taken over.

In the summer Wolf has himself signed off sick for three weeks and goes swimming. One day policemen are standing outside his door and want to take him away. It turns out that his mother and sister have taken a holiday at the same time. A neighbour in Berlin has noticed that the two women are away. The neighbour assumes they have fled to the West, whereupon the police call Wolf's workplace to check if he's still there. When he is missing too, a search is launched for the family, although this has to be quickly cancelled because Wolf is there and his mother and sister are demonstrably lying in the sun on the Baltic coast. This event brings him back to reality, particularly since he later receives another visit from the police, who immediately arrest him. This is because just before he left Berlin he and his friend Manfred threw a heavy wooden plank off the Flatow Tower in Potsdam. He was accused of damage to property, although this was withdrawn a short time later on grounds of insignificance.

All these stories involving the police have also attracted the attention of the army. Wolf receives his call-up papers, and has to report to Berlin immediately. At three o'clock in the morning he is standing along with 200 other young men in an empty car park outside the district military headquarters, which is based in a freshly assembled cardboard shed on Nordmarkstrasse. It is dark and cold, street lamps bathe the car park in pale light. They stand in the car park for hours. When dawn rises, a captain divides them into groups of five, and then they march to the station. Wolf is tired, he isn't used to getting up early, certainly not as early as this. He thinks about his girlfriends, about the warm bed in his room in Leipzig. It's only now that he understands that the fine life is over for the time being. The state has taken him in, to turn him into a Socialist. He feels cramped and confined. No more hide-and-seek from now on. He has been handed over to these men in uniform, to these yelling idiots who even seem to enjoy all this army nonsense. Wolf trots along behind the others, sees the familiar streets, the city waking up. He's glad he's not going to bump into anyone he knows from his other life at this time of day. Under his arm he carries a cardboard box, in which he will later send his clothes home. Later, when he is himself a man in uniform, one among many.

Wolf is brought to Sanitz, near Rostock, to an anti-aircraft regiment. The barracks have been newly built, the National People's Army is still young and just beginning to grow. Some of the officers also served under the Nazis. The uniforms haven't changed much in the meantime. Wolf thinks of Werner, of his time in the war, which isn't actually all that long ago. The army doctor attests that Wolf's knees are not entirely fit for service, which means that he is given an office job, which could be worse. In the regiment they're looking for someone who can draw. Wolf volunteers, and is immediately asked to paint a mural for the new cinema. The commander wants a heroic soldier with a steel helmet and a machine gun, looking into the distance, confident of victory. Below the picture he wants the line, "We are defending our homeland." Wolf does everything exactly as they want it, he is praised and given a position as a staff soldier. He is also trained as a projectionist, and put in charge of the library.

Beside the projectionist's cabin there's a little room with a lockable door. Here Wolf listens to records, reads books, is able to forget the world of the barracks a little and be on his own. Wolf notices that the army actually works exactly in the same way as the GDR as a whole. Here too there are little free spaces, niches that you can disappear into. Here too the principle of giving and taking is in operation. Wolf leads his regiment to victory in the great unit drawing competition, so he doesn't have to take part in the exhausting manoeuvres. He paints brightly coloured partitions when a general pays a visit, and luckily nothing happens to him when it turns out that his new girlfriend has spent the night with him in the barracks. He enjoys this game, testing the boundaries. He doesn't mind painting ludicrous propaganda pictures if it means they leave him in peace. He sees the others who don't believe in the great cause, but who all join in. Wolf says it's all about the facade, that the state didn't really demand genuine belief. You didn't have to bend the knee or sell yourself, you just had to go along with the big spectacle of Socialism.

I wonder whether that was really the case. Whether you really noticed when you'd crossed your own boundaries, when the alien belief slowly and unnoticeably seeped into you. Or whether in the end the others determined the rules of the game. Perhaps all those free spaces and possibilities were just an illusion that distracted you from the fact that you were joining in. I too always had the feeling of actually being true to myself, while at the same time I knew what I had to do to avoid getting into trouble. This combination of cheeky thoughts and good behaviour, of little lies and a big truth, is quickly learnt and hard to shake off again. It's a survival strategy, a protection mechanism for people who can't make up their minds.

Again and again Wolf breaks the rules as if trying to discover at any price the point at which the others will finally react. He doesn't do it deliberately, it just happens to him, and he himself is usually surprised by his daring feats. He takes his girlfriend for a ride on his moped and is stopped for speeding, with no driver's licence and no leave pass. Military police bring him back to barracks in handcuffs, and he is to be accused of desertion. It turns out that Wolf hasn't sworn an oath to the flag. On the day of the swearing-in he had, as a precaution, rubbed stinging ointment on one of his eyes. His eye swelled up, and he was taken to a hospital in Rostock. As a result he avoided taking the oath, and no one could prosecute him for his crime. He was supposed to catch up on his oath-taking, but something had always intervened, so that after a year and a half Wolf left the army without ever swearing loyalty to the Republic. He skilfully dodged the issue without open refusal.

Wolf later entertained us handsomely with his army stories. I loved his adventure with the People's Army. Again and again he would imitate the lieutenant colonel's face when he found a pair of women's knickers in Wolf's bed. Again and again he told us how he had climbed over the barracks wall drunk at night. Every time he embellished the story a little more. I don't know how much of those anecdotes was true, and Wolf himself probably didn't know after a certain point. At any rate my father's military service always sounded like enormous fun to me, with Wolf a kind of uncontrollable clown who always made the others look a bit sillier than they already were. Today, in fact, I think Wolf was probably more like a clever fish that dreams about the sea, and forgets that he's still swimming in an aquarium.

I don't think Wolf was an especially political person at the time. He wasn't yet convinced that the system was wrong. He was more concerned with himself, with his needs, with his dignity. He didn't like being told what to do. He was allergic to other people's rules, he wanted to determine his own life. When he felt pressure from outside he grew stubborn. If someone got on his nerves he thumped him in the face. I always experienced him as a strong, independent person. As someone who insisted on his own independence. Of course that can quickly become political in a country in which the collective is in charge, in which the independent self is supposed to be done away with. But even the comrades probably understood how Wolf works. In his Stasi file it would later say he was critical, but not hostile. The freedoms he took seemed somehow normal even to me. Without him I'd probably never have become a Westerner.

After the army Wolf goes to study print and design. Most of the other students are women. Soon he finds his way back into his old, easy life. He has one woman he goes to the theatre with, one who cooks for him and one he goes to bed with. College isn't particularly demanding, because most of what he's taught there he can do already. At home he is spoilt by his mother and sister. For Sigrid he's become a kind of substitute husband, for his little sister a father figure. When he is twenty-three, the two-and-a-half-room flat becomes too cramped for him, and he moves to the shop in Prenzlauer Berg. Even today that still rankles with Sigrid.

Wolf starts working as a freelance graphic designer, which isn't easy because there's a paper shortage in the GDR and it's hard to get commissions. The little money that he has Wolf carries as a bundle of notes in his trouser pocket. Sometimes he has nothing left at the start of the month. He doesn't eat much, and even a tram journey becomes a financial burden. This insecurity worries him, he's nervous and his blood pressure goes through the roof. When he's worked up he falls over, when he's under stress he goes to sleep. He says this new freedom was lovely, but it also frightened him. Perhaps it all reminds him too much of the time after the war when the family had no money and nothing to eat. He lacks that underlying feeling of security, the absolute confidence that things will somehow keep going. I noticed that a lot later on. When he bought ten cans of potted meat and couldn't explain why he'd done it. When he stored tons of coal in the cellar in case things changed. When the Wall came down and it wasn't clear what was going to happen next, Wolf bought warm underwear for the whole family. He himself knew that it was nonsense, but he couldn't help it.

Wolf and Anne, 1969

Eventually even all the affairs become too much for him. He decides to split up with them all and concentrate his energies. The evening he parts from the last of his women, he visits his friend Hansi. He already has another guest, a beautiful, pale woman with long, dark hair who doesn't even notice Wolf at first, whose attention he has to struggle for, who has something shy and girlish about her, but also a resolute quality. She casts a spell on him, his good intentions are forgotten. When they walk through the snowy park and he takes her hand, it's as if it couldn't be otherwise.

7

Traces

A S A CHILD I IDENTIFIED PEOPLE according to their cars. I
didn't know my parents' friends by name, but I knew if they
drove a white Wartburg Tourist or a Lada 1500. Most of them drove
Trabants, so they were hard to tell apart. Sometimes I remembered
the colour or particular fittings, but in fact Trabant drivers weren't
particularly interesting. A blue Skoda with added foglights and a
fake leather cover on the steering wheel, on the other hand, made a
huge impression on me. As did a red Moskwitsch with a fluffy duck
on the rear-view mirror. But my absolute number one was a light-
brown Citroën Pallas GSA. It belonged to Gerhard. This car was like
a Ferrari in the GDR. My greatest joy was when my grandparents
came to visit and I was allowed to sit in the Citroën while the rest of
the family had a cup of coffee. I would sit behind the wheel for hours,
imagining I was Erich Honecker's chauffeur. No idea how I hit on that
one, perhaps it was because the car was so unbelievably luxurious and
could only be really worthy of a head of state. Sometimes Gerhard sat
next to me and we played pilots. I was the captain, which was why I
was allowed to turn on the engine and move the lever that made the
car glide soundlessly upwards. My Communist grandfather could not
have given me a stronger argument for the superiority of capitalism.

In the Citroën era, which was only briefly interrupted by a Peugeot phase, my grandparents were living in Paris. Gerhard was working there as a correspondent for *Neues Deutschland*. I only ever saw him at Christmas and in the summer holidays, when he brought us boxes of Lego, jeans and velvet jumpers. Gerhard was the Western grandpa, who could fulfil almost all desires. Wolf always got presents too, which is why I couldn't understand why he thought Gerhard was so stupid. There were a lot of arguments about Gerhard in our house. Wolf said he was a Stalinist, and when I asked what that was, Anne dismissed the question and changed the subject. I sensed that something wasn't right, but I didn't understand what the actual problem was. Sometimes I heard my parents arguing in the kitchen, and when I walked in they fell silent. When I asked what they were arguing about, Anne said it was about politics. At the time I thought politics must be a pretty stupid thing if it put everybody in a bad mood. Eventually Wolf stopped even coming when we visited my grandparents. I saw less and less of Gerhard too. When we met he seemed absent and remote. We stopped playing pilots or Erich Honecker's chauffeur. There were fewer presents as well. That was the time when I lost my grandfather.

I only knew my other grandfather from Wolf's stories. When Wolf was twenty, he broke off all contact with his father. There were no letters, no signs of life, nothing. I knew his name was Werner, that he often beat Wolf, and that he liked other women more than Grandma Sigrid.

When Wolf talked about Werner, he was sad and slightly help-less, which was why I was always glad when we were able to talk about something else again. Werner was a weird, shadowy figure as far as I was concerned. An evil stranger. That was also why I wasn't particularly keen to meet him. Werner wasn't one of us, and there was no reason to change that.

It was only after the fall of the Wall that Wolf thought it was time to talk to Werner again. Perhaps it was because everything was in a state of confusion anyway. All of life was starting over again, it was the end of final decisions, and even an ostracized father got another chance. I was quite excited when we climbed to Werner's flat in Pankow one winter afternoon. Standing in the doorway was an old man who looked strangely familiar to me. Werner has the same eyes as my father. Amused, quick eyes that dart back and forth and register everything. When we went into the sitting room, Werner told Wolf to turn out the light in the corridor. I couldn't help laughing. That damned sentence had accompanied me throughout the whole of my childhood. Wolf had always told us to turn the light out when we left a room. Because electricity is expensive, and because there's nothing worse than wasting money. Now my father himself had become a child again, obediently turning out the light in the corridor. Werner showed us his workshop. Everything looked exactly as it did in Wolf's studio. The tools were neatly lined up, the paper was in the right-hand corner of the desk. I reflected that you probably never escape your father, however far you might push him away. I understood that I'd known Werner for ages. That he's in my father and perhaps also in me. That you don't decide who your father is.

My two grandfathers never met. I don't know if they'd have had anything to say to each other if they had met. Still, they built the same state, they were in the same Party, perhaps they even believed in the same things at some point. And yet they would probably have remained strange to one another because their careers were so different, because fate had guided them in very different directions very early on.

When Gerhard is born in Berlin on 8 June 1923, the family sends out cards on handmade paper with their son's initials embossed in gold. Gerhard has two older sisters who frame the son and heir like angels in the childhood photographs. The sisters wear ruched dresses and have enormous silk slides in their hair, and Gerhard is also wrapped in a white dress that makes his delicate face look even gentler. At this time Gerhard's father Wilhelm and a partner run a big international law firm on the Kurfürstendamm. They have a nanny, a housekeeper and a chauffeur. Frieda, Gerhard's mother, is in charge of the household. She is from the Hamburg seagoing family Barents, who trace themselves back to the Dutch seafarer Willem Barents, who in the sixteenth century discovered the route to the North Pole that was later named after him. They're very proud of that in our family even today, which might have something to do with the fact that we've all got a lousy sense of direction. I constantly get lost even in my own part of town, and my mother would probably starve to death if she was left out in the city park. Perhaps our gift for orientation was used up to such an extent 500 years ago that there's nothing left for us.

Wilhelm is from a Jewish family that moved from Warsaw to Berlin in the eighteenth century, and whose sons became either doctors or lawyers. The family converted to the Protestant faith very early, and otherwise tried to eradicate the traces of their Jewish origins as best they could. Even the original family name, Levin, was shed and replaced by Leo, which to my ears doesn't sound particularly Prussian either. When Gerhard is three years old, the family moves to Rheinsberg, to a villa on the lake. Later Gerhard asks his father why they left Berlin, and Wilhelm says, "It was high time. I was well on

Wilhelm, 1945

Frieda, 1943

the way to becoming wealthy." But probably it's most of all because his clients—mainly the chairmen of major companies—and the legal manoeuvres he had to carry out on their behalf were not congenial to him. William explains to his son that he'd rather deal with simple people and also escape the hurly-burly of Berlin, where he doesn't even have time to play the piano. Wilhelm is an excellent pianist, and has often regretted not being a musician. In Rheinsberg the family stands around the big grand piano every evening. They sing songs by Schumann, Schubert and Hugo Wolf. Once Gerhard asks his father why they've only got a normal car, while their neighbour, a confectioner, drives a huge car with chrome fittings. Wilhelm replies: "What matters are scientific and artistic merits, money doesn't count."

In Gerhard's memory, Rheinsberg is a paradise. The little town with the famous rococo palace is surrounded by forests and lakes. In the summer they go for long hikes and boat trips. When Gerhard comes out of school, he goes to his father's office and if he has time they have serious conversations. Gerhard is allowed to sit in the heavy leather armchair that is actually meant for clients. They talk about literature and music. Sometimes Wilhelm recites a poem which Gerhard then has to learn by heart. In November 1927 a retired French general commissions Wilhelm to bring a case on his behalf. It isn't a particularly big one. A relatively unknown far-right agitator called Joseph Goebbels claims that he was tortured in 1920 as a German patriot, in the basement of the French military headquarters in occupied Cologne, in the presence of the general. It was from those tortures, Goebbels announces in public speeches, that he got the club foot that people mocked him for at the time. The hearing is taking place in a Berlin court. Wilhelm is able to prove without much difficulty that Goebbels has had his club foot since birth. He presents a photograph of the little Goebbels lying naked on a bearskin rug. With a club foot. There is also a school photograph showing Goebbels in the front row with his club foot. Wilhelm also presents the judge with a certified copy of the military papers of the plaintiff, who was exempted from military service in the First World War because of his club foot. The court sentences Goebbels to pay a symbolic franc as damages to the French general. Once the ruling has been given, Goebbels' lawyer walks up to Wilhelm and says in a menacing voice, "You, sir, will remember this day often and vividly."

Wilhelm doesn't take these words particularly seriously. Only a few years later, in autumn 1932, when the Nazis set about taking power, does he remember the trial. Once Gerhard listens in on a conversation that his parents are having in the drawing room, in muted voices. Wilhelm says, "They'll take their revenge as soon as they can." The conversations over dinner, which until then had been light and cheerful because Wilhelm liked to amuse the family with funny anecdotes, become serious. All of a sudden his parents are talking only about politics. It's all about whether the Nazis are going to take over the government or not. Wilhelm calls the Nazis "Teutons", "barbarians" or even "the lawless ones", which is the most serious condemnation as far as he's concerned, because he places the law above everything else. Wilhelm has often told Gerhard that man is different from the animals primarily because he deliberately applies laws and thus creates a just coexistence. Wilhelm can't imagine that people who openly declare that they're not going to adhere to the constitution could ever enter government.

On 30 January 1933 Hitler is appointed Reich Chancellor. Only a few days later some boys in Gerhard's class are wearing brown shirts and swastika armbands. A schoolfriend tells Gerhard rather embarrassedly on the way home that he isn't allowed to play with him any more because Gerhard isn't racially pure. "Your mother is

Aryan, but your father is a Jew." Gerhard doesn't understand what his friend means. He's heard of Jews, but what does Aryan mean? Perhaps, Gerhard thinks, the boy's got mixed up. Does he mean Arabian? Gerhard has just read a book of adventure stories in which Arabian warriors gallop through the desert and defeat everyone who tries to stand up to them. He runs home, charges into his father's office and says he wants to be Arabian, like Mutti.

Wilhelm interrupts his work, invites Gerhard to take a seat in the heavy armchair and listens. Then his father tells him that the Nazis want to bring back times long past in which people were burnt on pyres for their origins or convictions. "Now nothing will be as it was," says Wilhelm, and for the first time Gerhard sees something like fear on his face. Gerhard must promise to tell his father anything that strikes him as strange. He should be extremely careful in conversations with teachers and other children. He is nine years old.

The night after the Reichstag fire, on 28 February 1933, a truck of armed SA men stops outside the family's house in Rheinsberg. Gerhard wakes up because he hears voices and shouts. He opens his nursery window and sees his father being beaten up by men in uniform and dragged through the front garden to the truck. He sees his mother, with tears running down her face, standing by the steps to the front door. Gerhard screams into the night. It is a desperate, piercing cry that sounds very strange even to him. He will see the pictures of that night before his eyes often in years to come. They are the pictures which shook him out of childhood, which will later show him time and again what is right and what is wrong. In his memoirs, which Gerhard wrote in the late Seventies and which, now that he himself can no longer speak, are my most important source for finding out things about his life, Gerhard writes: "Since I saw my father being abused by SA men as a child, the cruelty of the regime, its crimes against humanity, are my chief motivation for anti-fascist resistance."

I found the first version of his memoirs in a green file in the Federal archive in Berlin-Lichterfelde. Two hundred and ninety-eight typed pages, thin, yellowish copy paper that smells of dust when you turn the pages. My grandmother Nora probably typed it all out. For many long years she was his secretary and companion. I don't know if she wouldn't have liked to do something for herself. Whether he ever asked what she wanted. Nora was there when Gerhard needed her, she looked after the children and the household. She lived her whole life in his shadow, and she says today that that was fine. But then what is she supposed to say?

Gerhard always wrote by hand. He said he couldn't feel the text otherwise. His memoirs are archived in the files of the Central Party Control Commission. That was where the Party watchdogs sat, making sure that a comrade was still on the right path. The Commission also decided who was excluded from the Party, which for convinced comrades amounted to a death sentence. I would like to know how Gerhard's manuscript ended up there. Did he deliver it to the censors himself? Most of the text is identical to what was published a few years later under the title *Early Train to Toulouse*. But some passages have disappeared. Above all the one about the relationship between the German Communists and the Social Democrats in France. Gerhard describes cordial co-operation, but later on that didn't fit with the historiography of the East Berlin comrades. The violent debates among German émigrés in Paris about the non-aggression pact between Hitler and Stalin in 1939 don't appear in the book either. Gerhard writes about how shocked the German Communists were that Moscow should enter into a pact with the Nazis. But afterwards nobody wanted to remember that, because the German Communist Party had spoken in favour of the pact. And of course the Party never made a mistake.

In his account of his childhood and early youth Gerhard still displays feelings. He writes about his anxieties, his doubts, his weaknesses, his curiosity. Later, when he writes about his illegal work in France, when he himself must already have been a comrade, he just writes coolly and pragmatically. As if at some point something in his attitude had frozen and he could no longer change it. An attitude based entirely on appearance, which made even the most difficult decisions simple. Because it was no longer about him, but about the great cause whose servant he had become. I wonder whether he would still write it like that today, whether his attitude would have held. If he could still speak.

8

Stage Sets

O NLY WEEKS AFTER WILHELM'S ARREST the family learns that he was sent to Oranienburg concentration camp. Gerhard's mother pulls out all the stops to get her husband freed again. She calls the writer Ernst Wiechert, who is a good friend of Wilhelm's. Wiechert is held in high regard by the Nazis because he has not, unlike most of his colleagues, opposed them from the outset. Goebbels has a particular weakness for the author, and complies with his request to release Wilhelm temporarily from the concentration camp. Wilhelm spends some weeks in hospital. When he comes home again, Gerhard sees a pale, weakened man.

Goebbels takes on a lawyer to prepare a new trial in which it will be proved once and for all that his club foot is indeed the result of torture in French headquarters in Cologne. Wilhelm is questioned several times. Early in September the SA confiscate his passport and tell him he is on no account to leave his house. A few days later at dinner Wilhelm asks if Gerhard would like to go with him to Berlin the next day. In the morning they have breakfast at six o'clock and take the car to the capital. Wilhelm visits colleagues to whom he hands over the files of trials that he himself will be unable to continue. In the evening they go to a hotel near the Brandenburg Gate. Wilhelm puts on a tuxedo and Gerhard the dark-blue suit that he only wears on very special occasions. It is only when they are in the car driving along Unter den Linden that Wilhelm reveals they are going to the opera. Wilhelm says this visit to the opera was actually planned for a few years later, as an introduction to the world of adults. "But we haven't got much time, so you'll be growing up today." Wilhelm looks at his son with serious eyes. Then he smiles and says they're going to enjoy themselves hugely.

They go to the restaurant at the Staatsoper. The waiters know Gerhard's father and nod to him politely. There is roast chicken and French red wine, of which Gerhard is allowed to drink half a glass. Wilhelm leans over to him and whispers: "Let's not say anything about our concerns. Waiters and restaurant walls have ears." After dinner they go to the opera. Verdi's *Ballo in maschera* is being performed. Wilhelm has hired a box. In the interval an elderly lady from the neighbouring box asks if the little fellow understands it. Gerhard is furious about the question, since he is already ten years old. But he's comforted when he hears his father saying, "My son understands everything." In fact Gerhard hardly understands anything at all. He is fogged with alcohol and excitement. He hears the music as if in a dream, and the stage sets drift past him like a colourful carpet. In the end he has trouble keeping his eyes open. But it's still a great evening. He doesn't know that these are the last moments of his life in the *haute bourgeoisie*.

The next morning Wilhelm explains the situation. He says they're going to go and see a colleague who will help them get safely abroad. Wilhelm says he had no other choice, because he can't win a second trial against Goebbels. "I wouldn't survive another stay in the concentration camp." The lawyer's office is near the house where Wilhelm lived during his time in Berlin. His study strikes Gerhard as decidedly luxurious in comparison to his father's. There are thick carpets, deep, white leather armchairs and furniture made of steel and glass. A big glass facade looks out over the busy Kurfürstendamm. The lawyer greets Wilhelm like an old friend and suggests sending "the little fellow" out during the conversation. Wilhelm says, "My son is in the picture, and very discreet." Again Gerhard is incredibly proud. He likes this new time of secrets, this world of adults. He senses that a great danger is lurking behind all this, but he enjoys it anyway.

The lawyer explains that he's about to call in a man who was once the "king of smugglers" between Germany and Belgium. Now that the new government has intensified border checks, he uses his good contacts to smuggle people. The man owes him a favour, the lawyer says. So the price of his services is only 5,000 marks, a fifth of what he would normally charge. Half of it has to be paid immediately, the rest after their escape. The smuggler king is an elegantly dressed, good-looking young man. When he greets Gerhard, he winks at him as if they'd known each other for ages. He says he came back from Aachen during the night, everything's ready, but it must happen at the weekend. Wilhelm agrees, and starts counting out 100-mark notes on the table. The smuggler gets half of them, the other half goes to the lawyer. The lawyer takes a white sheet of paper out of his desk drawer and tears it into two unequal pieces. He gives Wilhelm one half of the sheet, and keeps the other with the money. "As soon as you're in Liège, give your companion your half of the sheet. If he brings it to me and it fits the other half, he'll get the rest of the money." The smuggler names a train that will take the family to Aachen on Saturday. The meeting point is the café at the main station.

Two days later Gerhard leaves the house in Rheinsberg at dawn along with his parents. His two sisters are already with their grand-mother in Hamburg and are going to come on later. They walk to the station on paths through the fields; they each have only a small briefcase, they've left everything else behind. In Berlin they stay with friends and the next day they take the train for Aachen. They are all very excited, but the journey is uneventful. In the café at the main station in Aachen two heavily made-up women are standing at the bar drinking schnapps. The smuggler isn't there. After a wait that strikes Gerhard as endless, he arrives at last. He apologizes for the delay. "I just wanted to be sure that no one followed you." They board the tram, switch lines several times and at last reach the end of the line, among fields outside the city. They cross a meadow and on the edge of the forest they see a high wire fence, the new forti-fied border. At one point there is a narrow opening with a turnstile. Beside it stands a sentry in field grey, holding a rifle. Wilhelm stops with horror when he sees the soldier, but the smuggler reassures him: "The man has had his money already." The soldier sees the new arrivals, puts his rifle over his shoulder and strides slowly along the fence towards the forest. They pass through the turnstile one by one. After about a hundred metres the smuggler says, "So, we've done it. We're in Belgium." He walks more slowly now and takes a deep breath as if he's just made a big effort.

Gerhard is a bit disappointed because everything here actually looks exactly like Germany. The Belgian forest is no different from the German, and the meadows along the border are like the ones at home. They reach a garden restaurant called "Le Coq jaune". There they take their leave of their companion. Gerhard is hugely excited, crossing the border without a passport is an incredible adventure for him. It's just a shame that he can't tell anyone about it. He notices with amazement that his parents look very gloomy. Only much later does he understand that at that moment they were probably thinking about their lost homeland and the uncertain life in exile that now lay ahead of them.

From Liège they travel via Brussels to Paris, where there is a rich relative who has promised to help them. Wilhelm puts all his savings together and rents a shop on Rue Meslay, near the Place de la République. There he sets up a Franco-German bookshop which will soon become one of the meeting points of German émigrés in Paris. The family lives in two small rooms that belong to the shop. By now the sisters have arrived from Hamburg, and their new home is getting cramped. Gerhard doesn't like Paris. He misses his friends in Rheinsberg. He longs for the swimming spots on the lake, his bicycle and his fox terrier Bruno. He can't talk to anybody in Paris because he doesn't speak French. Once, in the park, he sees an elderly lady having a lengthy conversation with her dog. He thinks even the dogs understand more than he does in this city.

A few weeks after their arrival in Paris Gerhard develops diphtheria. He is taken to the big children's hospital, the Hôpital des Enfants Malades, on Rue de Sèvres, where he is put in a ward with over forty children. The others are all chatting and laughing, and an older boy is telling funny stories that amuse even the nurses. Gerhard lies there mutely beside them. The ward doctor, a beautiful woman with short black hair and blue eyes, notices his loneliness. She sometimes comes to him and tries to cheer him up a little. On her rounds she spends a bit longer with him than she does with the others. When she examines him with her small, warm hands he feels as if an electric shock is going through his whole body. Gerhard doesn't really know what's happening to him, but when he sees that woman his heart pounds in his throat and all his worries flee. One day the doctor comes to his bed with a school book, an exercise book and a pencil and suggests that she give him a French-language lesson for an hour every day before she goes on duty. Gerhard is dizzy with joy, he works harder and more conscientiously than he ever did at school in Rheinsberg. The beautiful doctor sings him French children's songs and recites fables by La Fontaine that Gerhard still knows by heart today. Gradually he starts understanding what the other children are talking about, and by the time he is due to be released three months later he speaks French like a little French boy.

By now Gerhard is certain that he loves the doctor and wants to marry her when he's big enough. He wonders if he's allowed to say that to her, whether it isn't strange for a ten-year-old to court a grown-up woman. The night before his release he can hardly sleep, in the small hours he plans to see his declaration of love as a kind of test of courage. The doctor appears at the usual hour and he starts hesitantly, then faster and faster, telling her about his feelings. She listens to him seriously, doesn't even smile. When he's finished his declaration of love she thinks for a moment and says she likes him very much too. She's thirty-five years old and still unmarried, and if he's still willing to marry her in ten years' time and she hasn't yet found anyone else, she would live with him. Then she leans down to him, kisses him on both cheeks and leaves the ward. They see each other regularly for several months. She invites him to dinner in her flat, they go walking in the Bois de Boulogne or go to the cinema. But after a while they meet less often. Gerhard has joined a clique of boys at school, he has other things to do than meet a grown-up woman. One summer day in 1935 she says goodbye to him because

Gerhard in Paris, 1935

she has to move to a different town. They never see each other again. Later Gerhard told me about that first love, that woman who turned him into a Frenchman. He said there weren't many things he'd done in his life that he regretted. But that he could forget that woman so easily had always been a painful mystery to him.

In the summer holidays Gerhard goes to a camp for émigré children near Paris. Sleeping next to him is the son of Hans Beimler, the Communist who was already famous. He tells Gerhard how his father escaped from Dachau concentration camp and started his struggle against the Nazis. Gerhard asks the boy to tell him every last detail. He finds these stories so exciting that he decides to be like Hans Beimler one day.

After he gets back from the camp he tells his parents about his experiences and says, "I'm actually a Communist now." His father smiles when he hears that. He is sceptical about Communism, as he is about all extreme views. Wilhelm doesn't think much of the idea of destroying the whole bourgeois legal and state apparatus in order to put some peasants or proletarians in power. But he also sees that lots of Communists are fighting valiantly against the Nazis, and he thinks one should work with these people if one wants to bring down Hitler. Wilhelm lost his horror of the Communists early on. When, before the First World War, he was studying at the College of International Law in Geneva, he and one of his fellow students met a certain Monsieur Ulyanov in a café—a Russian revolutionary who would come to fame only a few years later under the name of Lenin. Lenin had patiently explained the politics of the Bolsheviks to the bourgeois young German, telling him that they considered terror against the Tsarist regime legitimate because the rulers also used terrorist methods. Wilhelm was very impressed by Lenin and was quite sympathetic towards the state he later founded. The coffee-house conversation with Lenin was also a reason why Wilhelm later considered joining the French Resistance, which also used violence to combat a violent regime.

Incidentally, the fellow student who took part in the conversation with Lenin in Geneva was Pierre Mendès-France, who became French prime minister after the Second World War. When Wilhelm arrives in Paris, Mendès-France is already an influential member of parliament with the ruling Radical Socialists. After the failure of the left-wing People's Front government in 1938, Wilhelm's family is ordered by the Paris police to leave the country immediately, along with many other dispossessed German émigrés. Wilhelm turns to his former fellow student for help. Pierre Mendès-France appears the very next day, buys up much of the stock of the bookshop and phones the French Minister of the Interior to persuade him to let the family stay.

Wilhelm is still the most important person that Gerhard can talk to about political matters. So for the time being Gerhard doesn't become a Communist, but a member of the "Faucons Rouges", the youth organization of the French Socialist Party. He wears a blue shirt and a red scarf and is present when the Red Falcons sing songs to thousands of workers on the shop floor of the Renault factory on the island of Seguin in the Seine during the strikes that paralyse the whole of France in 1936. Gerhard is also there in 1937 when the Falcons storm the Paris Mutualité and interrupt a speech by the Socialist Prime Minister Léon Blum with the cry "Planes for Spain". They are trying to persuade the head of government to support the Spanish Popular Guard in their struggle against the fascist Franco. But Léon Blum sticks to his policy of non-intervention in the Spanish Civil War and Gerhard wonders what sort of Socialists these people are if they don't dare to fight.

Along with his father he regularly goes to the Café Mephisto on the Boulevard St Germain, where the Association for the Protection of German Authors meets. They hear talks by Heinrich Mann, Lion Feuchtwanger, Anna Seghers and Rudolf Leonhard. The authors invoke the approaching end of the Nazi regime because, as they see it, a civilized people like the Germans will never follow these criminals. Their arguments sound so enlightening that Gerhard thinks the Nazis have actually been defeated already. One man who exerts a strong influence on the fourteen-year-old Gerhard is the great reporter Egon Erwin Kisch. He often comes into Wilhelm's bookshops and gives the émigré children lessons in German and history. At first Gerhard is most impressed by Kisch because he can do such virtuoso magic tricks. Kisch makes coins and matchboxes disappear in a flash, and sometimes they reappear in Gerhard's trouser pocket. Kisch can also talk as grippingly about historical events as if he had been there himself. Once he takes Gerhard and three other pupils to Versailles and shows them the settings of the French Revolution. They walk along the route that the furious Parisian market women walked in their protests against hunger. They see the throne of Louis XVI, and Kisch tells them about the cobbler who put that symbol of power in his workshop in the Faubourg St Antoine after the looting of the palace. For years the cobbler's customers were able to sit on the throne to have their measurements taken. Kisch tells stories very differently from school. He isn't interested in the lives of the kings, but in the revolts of the people. He looks at history from below and tells his pupils that all unjust regimes are condemned to be toppled by the proletarian masses. Now Gerhard is definitely determined to become a revolutionary, and when Kisch tells him the Communist Resistance fighters are definitely revolutionaries, his mind is made up.

One morning in April 1940 French gendarmes appear outside the front door at Rue Meslay and tell the family to pack up their belongings. The French government has issued an order for German refugees to be interned in camps, because France has, after all, been at war with Germany for eight months. This measure doesn't apply to Gerhard, because he isn't yet seventeen, and his mother is also exempt from internment so that she can look after him. Wilhelm and Gerhard's two sisters are put in a camp in Gurs on the edge of the Pyrenees. Gerhard suddenly has the feeling that he's losing his grip. He can't sleep at night, and even by day he lives in constant fear for his father and sisters. Everything that still seemed secure until then has become insecure. France, his new home, the land of democracy and human rights, has betrayed them. Bold thoughts race through his head. He imagines secretly freeing the family from the camp at night, shooting a guard who gets in his way. Then he feels sad and weak again. He knows now that there is no longer a safe place for him, that no one can protect him. He has to take control of his own fate.

9

Warnings

WHEN THE GERMAN WEHRMACHT nears Paris in June 1940, Gerhard packs a rucksack, says goodbye to his mother and leaves the city. He travels on foot, along with hundreds of thousands of Frenchmen who are all fleeing to the south of the country to escape the German soldiers. Railway transport has been interrupted, and the roads leading to Orléans and Lyon are all crammed. Heavily laden cars, trucks and horse-drawn carriages are trying to force their way through. Most people are on foot, like Gerhard. They are carrying suitcases and parcels, pushing prams. They walk hundreds of kilometres, passing through dead-looking towns and villages. By the roadside, vendors are selling old bread and bottles of tap water at inflated prices. When Gerhard nears Vichy, he learns of the capitulation of the French government under Marshal Pétain. He also learns that there is supposed to be an unoccupied zone in the south of France. Gerhard decides to keep on walking to the coast. He has only ever seen the Mediterranean in tourist posters and books, and it strikes him as a very pleasant place to escape to.

How quickly it all went, how few years lie between the end of his pampered childhood in Rheinsberg, life as an exile and now as a refugee. In his memoirs Gerhard describes this descent in a composed and sensible way: "It is true that the times are getting worse and worse, but things will keep going anyway." He doesn't complain, he doesn't wrangle with his fate. It may have something to do with his young age, or with the fact that he isn't the only one whose life is coming apart. Perhaps the many others with whom he fled from Paris made it easier to accept his own fate. But there's one thing he can't shake off: the feeling that he isn't really at home anywhere. I think Gerhard carried that feeling around with him for ages. It may even have been the most important reason for him to go to the GDR later on. To that country where so many homeless people sought a new beginning.

At the end of June Gerhard arrives in Cannes. The weather is wonderful, holidaymakers in pale-coloured suits sit on the terraces of the restaurants and cafés on the Croisette, white yachts bob in the marina, children play in the sand on the beach. It's all exactly as Gerhard imagined, but he himself feels a little forlorn. Just before Cannes he spent his last few francs on a pound of bread, he's quite dizzy with hunger, while on the promenade the smell of bouillabaisse reaches his nostrils. In the evening he discovers an abandoned tomato field in the hills above the city. There he finds another refugee from Paris who has been living on tomatoes for three days, and who suggests asking at the hotels, which are thought to be looking for part-time staff.

The next morning Gerhard walks along the backs of the hotels. He sees greengrocers and meat delivery men carrying baskets, boxes, sides of beef and whole calves into the rear entrances. By the entrance to the Grand Hotel there is a sign: "Kitchen boy wanted". In the staff office they tell him he can start as an unpaid apprentice. In return he can help himself to leftover food. The first time Gerhard steps inside the kitchen of the Grand Hotel he stands there as if enchanted.

He sees a huge, white-tiled room, with a whole battalion of spotless pots and pans boiling away on gas rings in the middle. He reports to François, a fat, congenial man wearing a pastry chef's cap, who congratulates him on his decision to learn the cook's trade. But first of all they have breakfast, because no one can work in a kitchen on an empty stomach. François, the head of patisserie and cold food, puts cold meat and pâté, a tin of sardines and various cheeses and cakes down on the table in front of Gerhard. Gerhard eats as much as he can and tells François, speaking with his mouth full, that he is a refugee from Germany. François advises him to keep that to himself, because it's not a good idea to mention foreigners here in the Grand Hotel, particularly when they come from Germany.

Work in the kitchen is hard. For ten to twelve hours a day Gerhard cleans vegetables and scrubs copper pots until the meat chef can see his stubble in them. He carries the heavy trays to the dumb waiter, cleans the floor, guts fish and cracks lobster shells. Along with four other kitchen boys, two lift attendants and a porter, he sleeps in a little room under the roof. It's unbearably hot at night, they only have a paraffin lamp and they have to fetch water in a bucket from the toilet. The pastry chef François reveals himself to be an anarchist, whose motto is, "If it's good enough for the moneybags in the dining room it's not good enough for us." When François has to make a special cake, he always produces two. The better one is for the employees. On one occasion a cream cake is ordered for the banquet of a Bolivian tin-mine owner. Gerhard carries the cake to the dumb waiter and trips on the way. The cake is dented on one side, there's ash stuck to the cream where it fell on the floor. Gerhard says gloomily that they'll probably have to deliver the other cake now. François resolutely rejects this idea, because at his table they don't eat anything that's been on the floor. François moulds the cake back into shape with his hands, reaches into the ashes and dusts the edge of the cake on all sides. "Tell the waiter I've made the cake in the Indian style this time," he says to Gerhard. Then the other cake is eaten in the kitchen.

The head chef, a fat, bald little man whom everyone addresses as "maître", only ever comes into the kitchen in a dinner jacket. Just before midday and half an hour before dinner he does a tour of the kitchen to check that his recipes are being followed to the letter. This tasting is a ceremony. The sous-chefs present him with sauces and pieces of meat on preheated plates. The soufflés and puddings are served up in ice-cooled bowls. Behind the master someone has to carry the tasting cutlery, and after three weeks this honour goes to Gerhard. Forks, spoons and knives are neatly aligned in a shallow morocco leather case. When the master brings something to his lips, there must be absolute silence in the kitchen. Then he pauses, quite motionless, shuts his eyes and gives his last instructions for the achievement of perfection. At the time the Grand Hotel in Cannes has one of the finest restaurants in France, and in spite of the horrendous prices the dining room is always full. So Gerhard gets to know the little dodges and the major differences in the art of cuisine. Even decades later he continued to celebrate it. When we had dinner at my grandparents', Gerhard always paid special attention to the meat. Sometimes he asked me to cut him a slice of the roast and tasted it with his eyes closed—as the master chef in the Grand Hotel had once done.

After a few weeks Gerhard is promoted to assistant waiter. He wears a white tropical tuxedo with black trousers and patent-leather shoes. Most of the guests are rich Americans and French members of the collaborationist government in Vichy. There is also a German who is there almost every evening. His name is Dr Müller, and he identified himself at reception as a representative of the German Red Cross. But a fellow waiter tells Gerhard he spotted the butt of a pistol under Dr Müller's left armpit when he was clearing up. He probably doesn't work for the Red Cross. One evening a senior American diplomat has his leaving banquet in Cannes. He comes in a convoy of cars from Paris, where the American Embassy has just been closed down. The party goes on into the night. Eventually the head waiter goes into a side room to rest. He tells Gerhard to call him as soon as the guests show signs of leaving. A few minutes after the head waiter has disappeared, the diplomat's wife, a slim blonde in pearls and diamond rings, gets to her feet. As she does so, her mink stole falls to the floor. Gerhard rushes over and lays the stole around her shoulders. She smiles, opens her handbag and puts a bundle of crumpled notes in Gerhard's trouser pocket. A few moments later the head waiter appears. He is furious because Gerhard didn't call him, and demands the tip. Gerhard thinks for a moment. He remembers that the personnel department told him to hand in his papers, he thinks of the hard, unpaid work and the money that would allow him to leave Cannes. He says no, and walks away. The waiter yells after him that he is fired, and must leave the hotel by seven o'clock in the morning. The next morning there's one last breakfast with François. He fetches a bottle of white Burgundy and truffled foie gras from the fridge. They drink to the future, and then Gerhard leaves the Grand Hotel, through the rear entrance, just as he arrived.

Via his mother, who is still in Paris, Gerhard manages to contact his father, who has escaped from the internment camp and is living under a false name in the village of Cazaubon near Toulouse. He is being looked after by an illegal Catholic aid organization. Gerhard heads off on foot. He only walks at night, because even in the unoccupied zone there are regular checks and raids now. Industrious

French gendarmes are hunting down Jews and foreign refugees, before handing them over to the Germans. After two weeks Gerhard reaches Cazaubon, and is able to hug his father for the first time in ages. Wilhelm has aged, his face has become narrow and transparent, and he has developed deep wrinkles around his mouth. Life in the camp, which he doesn't really want to talk about very much, has taken its toll on him. Wilhelm has a heart condition and has to take things easy. He can no longer manage more than one half-hour walk a day. This inactivity bothers him, because he would ideally like to be fighting the Nazis. But he has to leave that task to Gerhard, who has made contact with the Resistance via the husband of his sister Ilse. A few weeks later Kurt Weber, a former fighter in Spain who is now working with the Resistance in Toulouse, comes to Cazaubon. Kurt Weber tells Gerhard about the illegal work of the German Communists in France, whose chief task lies in spying on the Wehrmacht and recruiting German soldiers. He says Gerhard needs to be clear that he's risking his life if he joins the Resistance. He talks about torture by the Gestapo, about the death sentence awaiting anyone who gets caught. Someone like Gerhard, just nineteen years old, should think very hard about that. They agree to meet in Toulouse. If Gerhard comes, it means he wants to join.

At 1.30 in the afternoon on 12 May 1943, Gerhard is standing as agreed in the little park near the Capitole in Toulouse. He has to wait a few minutes before a small, broad-shouldered man appears from the shadows of an avenue and walks straight over to him. It is Werner Schwarze, code name Eugen. He suggests taking the tram out of town so that they can talk in peace. They travel through the southern part of the city past the gunpowder factory where the first shift is just getting out. Beyond the Garonne Bridge the tram stops outside a massive red-brick building surrounded by high walls. Eugen explains that this is the Fortress of St Michel, a prison from the previous century that the Germans are now using as a jail. Gerhard thinks that he might end up here if he makes a mistake one day. But he immediately dismisses the thought.

From the terminus a path leads into the vineyards that rise to the south of the city. Not far away a unit of German soldiers is driving along the road. From up here you can only see their steel helmets under the open tarpaulins of the trucks. The soldiers are singing songs, about flowers in an alpine meadow and a girl called Maria. Gerhard says he can't bear seeing all these German soldiers all over the place. Eugen smiles at Gerhard and says that he might be sitting on one of those trucks himself right now, if he'd happened to have a different father. Gerhard is startled by the comparison, and Eugen explains that lots of soldiers are opposed to the war, which is why it's important to engage with them, influence them and possibly even win them over to the right cause. Eugen's group distributes flyers in barracks and also produces an illegal newspaper in German called *Soldier on the Mediterranean*. Eugen says that many of the secretly distributed newspapers are immediately passed on by the soldiers to the Gestapo. But the rest are read, and passed around. "It's tiresome, exhausting work, but it might change something," says Eugen. Gerhard is a bit disappointed. He didn't actually want to distribute newspapers, he wanted to fight. But he doesn't say that.

Eugen's remark that it might be a matter of chance who fights on which side later preoccupies Gerhard. He wonders what would have become of him if they hadn't had to leave Germany, if his father hadn't been exposed by the Nazis by some kind of chance. He writes: "Personal dismay determined our path, but where would that path have led if we had been freer to make our own decisions?" It's almost as if he is relieved in retrospect not to have had a choice.

Eugen gives Gerhard the assignment of going into a German labour exchange and getting a job as an interpreter with a Wehrmacht unit. Gerhard gets an ID which was issued by a French town hall with a genuine official stamp, and which stands up to a thorough examination. His name is now Gérard Laban, he's seventeen, comes from Alsace and is a prospective student of German. He was born in Stenay near Verdun. The local *mairie* burned down in 1940, and the birth and death registers were destroyed, which makes it impossible to investigate his origins. He learnt the German language from his mother, which is why from now on he has to speak German with a French accent. Both his parents died young and his only relations live in Algeria. Eugen also gives him the address of an elderly couple with whom he can live in Toulouse. He warns Gerhard to be extremely vigilant at all times. Then they part.

In the German labour exchange his story works fabulously well. He is taken on as an interpreter in transportation headquarters, which is based in an old hotel right behind the railway station. His boss is Corporal Fink, who wears a tailor-made uniform that seems to be cut of very good cloth. Soon Gerhard learns that Fink's chief duty is to organize the Wehrmacht black market in unroasted coffee beans, which are taken from Toulouse to Germany by rail. Officially, Fink is responsible for relations between headquarters and the French authorities, which is why he urgently needs an interpreter. Fink is a likeable, uncomplicated type. He is so preoccupied with the black market that he soon leaves everything else to Gerhard, who now has access to all the written correspondence of the headquarters. He also gets hold of the transport plans which reveal the times of trains carrying prisoners or ammunition. Because it would be too difficult to make notes, he has to commit everything to memory. The routes, the departure times, loading, waiting times. Gerhard develops a mnemonic technique that enables him to keep all the details of up to ten transports in his head. At night he sits in his room at home and writes everything down in miniature handwriting on cigarette paper. A messenger comes twice a week and collects the secret messages.

Once Corporal Fink forgets to lock his safe, and Gerhard quickly flicks through the "Secret Service Matters", which do not appear in the regular correspondence. He finds an instruction from Lieutenant General Kohl in Paris, who is responsible for all the French transport headquarters. Kohl writes that from now on prisoner transports are to take "absolute precedence". The deportation "of Jews and terrorists" has highest priority. Gerhard sees the routes that the prisoner transports are due to take. The prisoners are collected in Drancy and Compiègne, and distributed in various directions from there. Their final destinations are Auschwitz, Theresienstadt, Ravensbrück, Dachau, Buchenwald. Eugen tells him there is information to suggest that Jews from all over Europe are being killed in great numbers in the Polish camps. There's talk of gas chambers, although no one knows if that's true. Gerhard doesn't believe these stories. Not even the Nazis would commit a crime like that, he thinks.

In Fink's secret documents Gerhard also finds a letter that was sent anonymously to the Wehrmacht. It says there is a waiter at the officers' mess at transport headquarters in Toulouse who works for the Resistance. He is called Gaillard, but his real name is Riedinger. In the margin of the letter there is a note from the head of security at transport headquarters: "Must be arrested immediately." The note is already two days old. Gerhard wonders if it's too late to save Riedinger, or whether Fink might have left the safe open deliberately to test him? Gerhard decides to do something. Immediately after close of business, he goes to a phone box and calls headquarters. Disguising his voice, he says that there's been an accident in Monsieur Gaillard's family, and he needs to speak to him urgently. When Gaillard finally comes to the phone, Gerhard says, "This is a friend. You're to be arrested, get out."

Several weeks later Gerhard learns from something that Corporal Fink says in passing that the waiter managed to escape. There is now great excitement in the Gestapo. They try to find the source of the leak. And ambushes by partisan units on prisoner transports are becoming ever more frequent. Through an open door, Gerhard hears a conversation between Corporal Fink and head of security Captain Wächtler. Wächtler says the ambushes are being planned deliberately, "as if the terrorists know exactly when the prisoner transports are travelling". Gerhard feels proud and elated, he now knows that his work has a purpose. At the same time he warns himself to be even more careful.

One morning Gerhard is woken by a loud knock on his bedroom door. It's only half past five in the morning. His landlady is standing outside the door, in a state of distress. She says a German soldier is standing outside the door downstairs and wants to speak to him. Gerhard wonders whether he should escape via the garden, but if he was going to be arrested, more than one soldier would have come. The landlady says the soldier claims to be a friend of Gerhard's. It turns out that this is Corporal Weininger, with whom Gerhard actually was acquainted. Weininger is the commanding officer's chauffeur. He stands breathlessly in front of him and says Gerhard must disappear straightaway because he's going to be arrested today. Weininger says he drove head of security Captain Wächtler the previous evening. He had been talking to another officer about how "this man Laban must be taken into custody". Weininger offers to drive Gerhard somewhere. Gerhard hides in the back of the big Wehrmacht limousine. He has Weininger drive to an address that

Eugen had given him as a safe house in emergencies. He gets out a few streets early, thanks Weininger and asks if he doesn't want to switch sides. Weininger looks at him in amazement and drives off without replying.

The safe house is a chemist's shop, still shut. Gerhard waits in a house doorway until the chemist, a squat, grey-haired man, finally opens the door. Gerhard explains why he has come and the man quickly pulls him into the shop. By day he must hide in the medicine storeroom, which smells of lotions and corn ointment. Eugen comes in the evening, wearing an elegant camel-hair coat and a dark suit because, as he says, he's never checked in that disguise. Eugen already has new papers for Gerhard. His name is now Jean-Pierre Ariège, and he is a seventeen-year-old office clerk. A new photograph has to be taken, and the job is done by an acquaintance of the chemist's. The next morning Gerhard boards a bus with Eugen, and they drive fifty kilometres north. They wander along little roads and country paths until they reach a house on the edge of the forest. Gerhard is to live there for a while, until they have decided what his new mission is to be. In the house he finds four former members of the Spanish Republican Army and two German émigrés who are waiting for their new mission, like Gerhard. In the evening the men light a fire in the hearth, one of the Spaniards has dug up a badger's sett and Gerhard prepares one of the animals. They drink red wine and talk. For security reasons they're not allowed to talk about their illegal work. Gerhard spends a week in the house at the edge of the forest. He likes being with people he can relax with. He is allowed to speak German without an accent again, even though it's no longer very easy.

*

Gerhard as a lieutenant in the French armed forces, 1944

I wonder what was happening in Gerhard at the time, what he thought about when he was able to relax. Didn't he have doubts or fears? Didn't he sometimes want just to stop, to run away, to escape this struggle? It was pure luck, after all, that he had escaped arrest. Did he not wonder what it would be like next time? His memoirs sound like the stories he told me or my mother. They are about a brave young man driven by a conviction. A young man who has no choice but to fight the enemy threatening his life and his family's. This young man knows no questions and no doubts. He fights. But was that really the case? Can a conviction be so strong that it simply makes disturbing emotions and weaknesses disappear? Or did he repress it all? Did he forbid himself to be weak?

Before Gerhard became a fighter, he was a delicate, sensitive youth. Someone who cried at sad Schubert *Lieder*. There is a photograph showing him in September 1944 in the uniform of a French lieutenant. He wears a beret and looks so dreamy and unmilitary that you would take him for a poet or a singer, but never for a soldier. The uniform looks like a disguise on him. In his memoirs Gerhard writes that after his escape to Toulouse the comrades offered to let him take a break so that he could deal with everything that had happened. He resolutely refused the offer and asked for a new mission, the sooner the better. He wants to be useful, successful, the struggle should be worth it. One of the questions that Gerhard keeps asking himself is whether what he's doing is enough, whether he shouldn't actually be doing much more. He feels so small and unimportant compared with this overwhelming enemy.

In the archive I've found an assessment that the go-between Eugen, alias Werner Schwarze, wrote about Gerhard. He writes that Gerhard is "too impatient, too impetuous, which is probably down to his great youth". Eugen praises Gerhard's courage and commitment. "But he lacks the fear that makes you cautious. He's inclined to force successes."

10

Mistreatment

I N MID-JANUARY 1944 Gerhard is sent to Castres, a small town
100 kilometres from Toulouse. There is a Wehrmacht division
stationed there, made up mostly of Soviet prisoners of war who are
to be deployed against the partisans in France. Gerhard's mission is
to make contact with the German officers charged with training the
prisoners. He is to find out how the officers assess the operational
capability of their unit. Eugen says it's a difficult mission, because
the Wehrmacht has only sent selected staff to Castres. If it's too
difficult, Gerhard should abandon the operation rather than take a
risk. "Caution is the first rule," says Eugen before taking his leave.

Compared with Toulouse, Castres is a very small town. It's easy
to get your bearings, but you also attract more attention. The Agout,
a narrow river, divides the town into two halves. There are four
bridges that you have to cross if you want to get through the town,
ideal places for ambushes. Eugen has given Gerhard the address of
a couple who work in a textile factory, and he can stay with them.
The house where they live is right on the river. In the evening, at
the agreed time, he knocks at the door on the second floor. Three
short knocks and one long one. It is opened immediately. His hosts
are called Noémie and Marcel; Gerhard introduces himself as

Paul. Over dinner the French couple talk about their work with the Resistance in Castres. For weeks they've been smuggling flyers into the barracks where the Soviet prisoners are being trained. There is contact with the prisoners, but not with the officers. Noémie and Marcel warn Gerhard to let things move slowly. The Wehrmacht has sent a whole counter-intelligence unit to Castres because they don't trust the prisoners.

Gerhard uses the first few days to look around the town. He finds out that the German officers meet in various restaurants in the evening, but above all in a bistro on Rue Gambetta near the theatre. Some stone steps lead to the cellar, where there are dark-stained wooden tables and benches. Here you can drink red wine from the Dordogne and Armagnac at black-market prices. From eight o'clock in the evening the bistro is always packed. Gerhard mingles among the guests, and after a few weeks the German regulars have got used to him. They talk about the weather, the high alcohol prices and their families at home. One evening Gerhard falls into conversation with a corporal whose name is Günther Wegener, and who talks openly about the state of the war, the threat of defeat on the Eastern Front and a possible American landing on the French coast. Wegener had been at the Front in Russia, was wounded and transferred to France. He says, "If only all this shit could be over soon," and gives Gerhard a challenging look. But Gerhard doesn't want to give too much away too quickly, so he changes the subject and tells funny stories about his schooldays in Paris. When they part company, Corporal Wegener says this has been the best evening he's had in Castres. They arrange to meet again three days later.

In the weeks that follow, Gerhard meets Wegener regularly. Once they go to the opera together and see *Tosca*. In the final act, when Tosca stabs the chief of police and sings, "All Rome trembled before him," a voice in the circle shouts, "And who does Castres tremble before?" The lights immediately come on and the curtain is lowered. The audience boo. After a while the director of the opera comes on stage and says the performance has been halted on the orders of the police because catcalling is forbidden.

Wegener seems very troubled after this event. The hostility of the French bothers him. He asks Gerhard what the people here would do with someone like him if they lost the war. The two men go to the bistro near the theatre. After a few glasses of wine Wegener talks about the Eastern Front. Once he drove through a burnt-down village in a cross-country vehicle. A child of about three sat crying among the charred ruins. Wegener stopped the vehicle and jumped down to rescue the child. But a lieutenant sitting next to him shouted at him to leave the Russian brat where it was. Wegener talks about men, women and children being driven to cattle trucks through a snowstorm. "Like animals," he says, and falls silent.

Gerhard decides to give Wegener a flyer about the Wehrmacht's war crimes in France and the Soviet Union. He says he found the flyer in the street, and is about to take it out of his pocket when the door bursts open and three German military police storm into the bistro, sub-machine guns at the ready. They come up to the table where Gerhard and Wegener are sitting and the leader says to Gerhard, "You're under arrest. If you try to escape, you will be shot." The police push Gerhard to the door. The street outside is deserted. Fifty metres to the right are two black Citroëns with their engines running. Gerhard is pushed into the back of the first car, then the cars roar off. Gerhard sees it all as if through a veil, the houses which they speed past, the uniforms of the two guards he is wedged between. He thinks of the flyer in the inside pocket of his jacket, of his fake ID. He knows that the Gestapo torture prisoners with electric wires and red-hot irons to force them to talk. He feels his whole body suddenly becoming cold and numb. He could weep with fear, but he controls himself.

The cars drive into the barracks yard, and Gerhard is led into a guardroom. Several officers are standing around a desk, and among them is Wegener, who has just picked up the phone and is speaking very calmly into the receiver: "Lieutenant Colonel, we've got him." Gerhard's pockets are searched, and they find the flyer. Gerhard is led to an office on the first floor. Behind the desk, under a lamp with a green shade, sits a man with white hair and red eyes. An albino. He is the lieutenant colonel of the Wehrmacht counter-intelligence service. The albino holds the flyer in his hand and asks how much Gerhard is being paid to distribute these flyers. Without thinking, Gerhard says, "You don't do something like this for money, you do it out of conviction." He's immediately annoyed with himself for this unconsidered answer, because he has now needlessly admitted to distributing illegal flyers. Gerhard firmly undertakes not to say anything else that might be significant, and above all not to betray anybody, not to give away any names or accommodations, however severe the torture.

The albino asks about his go-betweens. Gerhard describes some-one who is the exact opposite of Eugen. Small, dark-haired, bald. He says he had only met the man, who called himself Maurice, in the street. The albino laughs: "So, the great unknown." He asks about the flyers that have been distributed in Castres. Gerhard confesses to distributing them all, because he knows it makes no difference in the end whether you've distributed one flyer or hundreds. The albino looks very pleased and says that means the question of the flyers is now resolved. He has Gerhard led away by the military police. They take him across the yard to a one-storey building with small, barred windows, and one of them opens the iron doors. When Gerhard is about to go in, a policeman's fist lands in his back, knocking him to the stone floor of the cell. Before he can get back up again, the other policeman is over him, kicking him in the ribs with his boots. Gerhard struggles for air, tries to protect his head with his arms. Just then terrible shouts are heard from the neighbouring cell. "Shut it, you Russian swine," roars one of the policemen. They let go of Gerhard and kick the other cell doors. The door falls closed behind Gerhard, and the bolt slides shut. He is alone in the tiny cell. Under the window there is a narrow plank bed with a dirty horse blanket. Next to it is an empty preserving pan that probably serves as a toilet. Gerhard stretches out, shaking, on the pallet. Now he has time to think.

He wonders why the albino didn't try to force the names of his comrades from him. He must have known that the first hours after arrest are the most important for getting confessions, because lots of clues could have disappeared the next day. Perhaps it's enough for the albino to have resolved the issue of the flyers. Perhaps he isn't going to torture him or hand him over to the Gestapo, who are said to be much more violent than the Wehrmacht. Gerhard reflects that he actually knows far too much about the work of the Resistance. He knows so many names and addresses. He would really like to be able to forget about them all. Again he starts having doubts about whether his work has had any value at all, whether he has actually achieved anything worth mentioning. He knows he's made mistakes, he knows he's acted too quickly again. Was Wegener a counter-intelligence spy who'd been set on him? And what would Eugen think about his arrest? The bell in the nearby church tower strikes midnight, the full moon illuminates the dark walls of the cell, which are covered with inscriptions. He makes out some Cyrillic letters. One of his predecessors in the cell has carved a Russian farmhouse surrounded by trees into the wall. Gerhard doesn't fall asleep until the small hours. But the albino pursues him even in his dreams. He is sitting on his desk, staring at him with his red eyes, pulling on his tongue with some strange piece of equipment. Little pieces of paper covered with all his secrets fly from Gerhard's mouth. The albino laughs and tugs harder and harder until the whole room is filled with the pieces of paper.

Gerhard spends the next day in his cell. A few Russian prisoners sing melancholy songs. A corporal opens the cell door and throws in a piece of bread. The following day he has to pay another visit to the albino, who knows by now that Gerhard worked for almost a year at transport headquarters in Toulouse. On the desk in front of the albino is a record of the first interrogation. Gerhard can read a few sentences. The last paragraph says: "Two intensified interrogations have produced no new information."

Intensified interrogation means torture. Why is the albino lying to his superiors, why is he sparing him? The albino flicks silently through Gerhard's papers, sometimes shaking his head, once even smiling. He says the matter will be heard before a court martial in Toulouse, he has a friend there, and he will inform him about it. Gerhard is led away, the albino nods encouragingly at him

It is only years later that Gerhard thinks he understands the counter-intelligence officer's behaviour. The Wehrmacht Secret Service was about to be dissolved at the time. The head of counter-intelligence, Admiral Canaris, was one of the conspirators who carried out the attempt on Hitler's life on 20 July 1944. For the SS this was a welcome opportunity to get rid of the service, which had been seen as a millstone for a long time. It could be that the albino has more important things to do in his last few days on duty than force confessions from partisans.

At dawn the next day, Gerhard is fetched by a sergeant and a private. The sergeant cuffs Gerhard's hands behind his back. "Do anything at all and I'll shoot you," he says. Then Gerhard is shoved into a Wehrmacht limousine and the drive to Toulouse begins. On the country road they are overtaken by a motorcycle with a sidecar. The sergeant draws a gun and winds down the window. He doesn't relax again until the motorcycle has passed. In Toulouse the streets are full of people. In the distance Gerhard sees the red-brick building of the St Michel prison. When they reach the big portal, the sergeant passes the duty soldier a piece of paper through the window, and the car drives into the yard. Gerhard thinks of his first walk in Toulouse with Eugen, when they passed the prison on the tram. How optimistic and naive he had been back then.

His days in prison are all the same. At six o'clock in the morning a corporal in the hall shouts, "Get up." There is a piece of army bread and a cup of ersatz coffee. After breakfast every prisoner is allowed to walk in the courtyard for twenty-five minutes, and wash at one of the taps. At midday a bowl of turnip soup is pushed through the hatch in the cell door, in the evening there's a piece of margarine or cheese substitute. On the fifth day Gerhard is fetched from his cell. "Interrogation," says the warder. Gerhard is led to a room where Captain Wächtler, the head of security of transport headquarters in Toulouse, is sitting at a table. Two SS men stand on either side of him. Gerhard's heart pounds with fear. "Who would have thought we would meet again so soon?" Wächtler says quietly. One of the SS men takes a pair of black leather gloves from his pocket and pulls them slowly over his hands.

"What's your real name?" asks Wächtler. "Gérard Laban, Jean-Pierre Ariège, Gérard Lebert, quite a lot of names." Gerhard says nothing and receives his first blow to the head. Everything goes black, and he falls off his chair. When he gets back up he gets a second blow to the stomach, then both SS men lay into him. Gerhard feels kicks in his belly and his ribs. Blood flows from his mouth. He can barely breathe. The SS men stop beating him up, Gerhard looks up at Wächtler, who is bright red with fury and shouting at him to tell him everything because there's no point denying it. Wächtler wants to know who warned the waiter Gaillard from the officers' mess about his forthcoming arrest. Gerhard says he doesn't know anyone called Gaillard. Wächtler gives the SS men a sign, and they tear into him again. At that moment a young lieutenant comes into the room. He tells Wächtler that intensified interrogations are not allowed in prison. He insists that the prisoner be brought back to his cell immediately. Wächtler is furious, but the prison officer sticks to his ruling. He has Gerhard brought to a one-man cell in the basement, and calls a paramedic. The warder, a grey-haired corporal, takes Gerhard's arm and lays him carefully on the pallet. "Have yourself examined," he says. "It doesn't look good, but I've seen worse, much worse. I'll get you your plate and your blanket." The paramedic establishes that his upper incisors have been broken, his lung is burst and five of his ribs are broken. "It'll all be OK," he says.

Gerhard never told either me or my mother anything about this interrogation in St Michel prison. He wrote about it in his memoirs, but none of us dared to talk to him about it. Perhaps we wanted to spare his feelings, which might have turned a strict grandfather into a weeping man. I was fourteen when I first read his book about his time in France, and I couldn't believe that he had had to endure all that. That he was the man who had doubled up, bloody and fearful, under the boots of the SS men. And who still didn't say anything. I only understood how brave he had been when I was arrested myself. That was on the evening of 8 October 1989, a day after the fortieth anniversary of the GDR. Along with my friend Christine I was arrested by two Stasi in Alexanderplatz. We were carrying flyers for the "New Forum", and were put on a truck that brought us to a police barracks. There we had to spend all night standing in a cold garage. The next morning we were questioned separately. I was very frightened, because I really had no idea what was going to happen to us. The interrogator just had to raise his voice once and I told him everything I knew. Gerhard didn't say anything, even though his life was in danger. I gave in, even though there wasn't actually anything much to be afraid of.

I I

Hostilities

AFTER GERHARD'S MISTREATMENT by the SS men the warder brings double portions of food to Gerhard's cell, and suddenly there are even a few bits of meat in the turnip soup. Gerhard can't yet walk, and spends hours dozing on his pallet. He imagines the Allies have landed and are on their way to Toulouse right now. The first thing they will do after their arrival, of course, is liberate the prison. They take him from his cell, and everyone cheers and dances, and in the evening they drink wine, and there is bread, as much as you can eat. Soon Gerhard is taken to a cell already occupied by three young Frenchmen who give him suspicious looks because he speaks German to the warden. In the evening they lie in silence on their beds, and one of the three Frenchmen starts whistling a tune. Gerhard recognizes the song of the Red Falcons. When the other man's whistling falls silent, Gerhard whistles the tune to the end. The Frenchman asks how Gerhard knows the song, and eventually they work out that they were both at the Red Falcons' camp in Villeneuve in 1936. The suspicion vanishes, and Gerhard is welcomed with open arms by the Frenchmen. They have been developing escape plans for weeks. They have woven a rope from bed sheets and smuggled a knife into the cell, so now all they need is a hook with which they can fasten the rope to the prison wall. They tell Gerhard of their plans. It sounds dangerous, but Gerhard would do anything to get out of this prison now. He thinks of the Count of Monte Cristo, who also escaped from a fortress. It used to be his favourite book. But he's not sure if real life works like that.

In mid-May Gerhard is taken away by two military policemen, who are to bring him to the court martial. They drive through the dense Toulouse traffic. The weather is fine, the women are wearing thin dresses, people sit chatting on the café terraces. Gerhard is disappointed, life just goes on as if nothing had happened. He knows that in a few hours he will probably be sentenced to death, and then the only question will be when he faces the firing squad. Gerhard has heard of a prisoner who was sentenced to death in January and is still alive. He thinks of the execution, of what it will be like when the bullets pierce his body. The thought makes him shiver on that warm day.

They drive to the Capitole, the city hall, a magnificent eighteenth-century building, with a massive keep on its southern side. The court martial is in one wing of the city hall which is guarded by soldiers. When Gerhard gets out of the car in the courtyard, he is approached by a young lieutenant who introduces himself as his counsel. The lawyer has an open, likeable face. He has read Gerhard's files and he has a few ideas about how to delay the trial. The lieutenant advises Gerhard to claim he was expatriated by the Germans in 1935. In that case the trial would not be brought against a Reich German, but against a stateless man. And he should remember whether Corporal Wegener, who betrayed him in Castres, didn't mention his connections with the Resistance several times. "The trial papers would have to be rewritten, investigations would have to be carried out, and that could take months," says the lieutenant.

Gerhard asks why he's doing all this for him, and the lieutenant says he has a friend in Castres who sends his greetings. "The albino?" asks Gerhard. "Yes, that's what they call him," the lieutenant says with a laugh. Gerhard is confused by the German officer's kindness. He thinks about how many members of the Wehrmacht have helped him over the past few months, and he thinks about Eugen's words, that you shouldn't just condemn all these men in uniform out of hand.

The courtroom is panelled with dark wood, and huge chandeliers hang from the opulent stuccoed ceilings. Shortly after Gerhard has sat down on the defendant's bench the judges appear, and everyone has to rise. The presiding judge is a general with a gaunt face, a thin hooked nose and a monocle that makes him look like a caricature from the days of the Kaiser. The charges are: deliberate subversion of the German armed forces, evading military service and high treason. The prosecutor, a colonel, delivers a long speech about Gerhard's activity in treasonous organizations, about the huge damage that he has done to the German armed forces with his actions. All of a sudden Gerhard has the feeling that he hasn't been all that unimportant after all. His defending counsel takes the floor and speaks of Gerhard's supposed expatriation, and he also requests that Corporal Wegener be brought in for questioning because there is a suspicion that Wegener could also be a traitor. The presiding judge is impatient, but he adjourns the case. Not least because he considers the charges so serious that a higher court should actually be ruling on them. When Gerhard hears of the adjournment the tension leaves his body, and he smiles at his counsel. The presiding judge sees that and roars at him, "Be under no illusions, the only possible punishment for what you've done is the death sentence."

A Belgian officer is brought to the cell next to Gerhard's in St Michel prison, on charges of spying in France for the British. Gerhard is able to talk to him through the open windows. The Belgian talks about the state of the war. The Allies are already close to Rome, he says, and a new offensive by the Red Army is under way on the Eastern Front. The Allied landing in France was planned for the first week of June in Normandy, the Belgian says. Gerhard looks at the calendar that he has scratched in the cell wall. There are another three weeks until the beginning of June. On the morning of 1 June Gerhard tips his bed against the window and climbs up on it. The piece of sky that he can see is blue. But what is the weather like at the coast almost 900 kilometres further north? The Belgian says it all depends on the sea crossing: if the waves are too high the boats won't be able to land.

The weather stays good in Toulouse, but there is no news of the landing. By now Gerhard knows that he could be shot even without a new trial. That recently happened to a prisoner on his corridor. His trial had also been adjourned, and the firing squad still came to get him at night. "They're going to shoot me," he yelled when the military police dragged him down the corridor. Since then Gerhard has slept uneasily, the slightest noise wakes him up. When he hears footsteps in the corridor he lies there drenched in sweat. He stays awake until the pale moonlight shimmers through the window. It's only when the metal cans of ersatz coffee rattle down the corridor that he calms down again. He's made it through another night.

On the afternoon of 3 June 1944 they come to get him. The soldier who cuffs Gerhard's hands behind his back says he's going to be taken to Fresnes near Paris. To the Supreme Court Martial. Gerhard reflects that Paris is at least closer to the north coast than Toulouse. They drive to the station in a black Citroën with SS runes on the number plate. Gerhard is surprised to note that they do not use the entrance for military trains, but the one for normal passengers. His escorts guide him through the crowd waiting for the express train to Paris, which has just pulled in. In the middle of the train there is a carriage with the inscription "Wehrmacht only". Gerhard remembers a report he read at transport headquarters, which said that military carriages should be included in normal trains to reduce the risk of violent attack. The front compartment of the carriage is occupied by five military police, who take charge of Gerhard.

Gerhard sits wedged between two military policemen. The train rarely travels at normal speed, it rattles along at a leisurely pace. Just before Montauban, about sixty kilometres from Toulouse, the train stops in the open countryside. The military police ask a blue-uniformed German railwayman the cause of the stop. "Terrorist activity," says the railwayman. The military police take turns to sleep, and at least two of them always keep their eye on Gerhard. In the afternoon they pass Cahors. The sun shines, Gerhard sees fields and stretches of forest, the mountains become steeper, and soon they are in the Massif Central. The train stops at a little station. A voice calls out, "Allassac, would all passengers please disembark, the train ends here." The doors of the other carriages open, the passengers stream out and pass through the barriers. Soon the platform is deserted again. The military police become nervous. "Shit," says one of them. "Right in the middle of bandit country." Two men are sent off to ask what happens next. Soon after that shots ring out, and they both run breathlessly back. They are talking about men with machine guns standing in the station building. Gerhard is electrified. The partisans are there! The sergeant major in command of the troop looks at him and says, "Don't get your hopes up. Before we have to get out of here we'll put a bullet in your head." He is interrupted by a violent explosion. One of the military policemen has to go out onto the platform and find out what's happened. The locomotive boiler has been blown up, he breathlessly reports a few moments later. There is the sound of fighting from the town. Machine-gun fire, long salvoes, followed by a huge explosion. "An anti-tank grenade," says one of the policemen. "But not one of ours," says the sergeant major. Two military police guard the window overlooking the tracks, two others the side towards the platform. A few moments later the first bullet flies into the compartment. The military policemen shoot back. But outside it's got dark in the meantime, and they can't see anything. "Stop shooting," yells the sergeant major. But the shooting outside has stopped. All of a sudden it's so quiet that they can hear the crickets chirping, through the shattered window there comes the smell of new-mown hay. All of a sudden something happens on the platform. The sergeant major tells Gerhard to shout in French, "This is the German Wehrmacht, who is there?" Gerhard shouts. In reply a salvo of machine-gun fire hits the roof of the carriage. A clear voice calls back in French. "We'll show you who we are, you bastard." Gerhard is happy to translate.

As soon as it is light, a new attack begins. Shots from sub-machine guns, carbines and a light machine gun ricochet around the compartment. Gerhard is told to lie on the floor. One military policeman is injured in his left hand, another has a graze on his head, blood seeps through the bandage. Gerhard creeps slowly along the floor of the corridor. Suddenly the whole carriage is shaken by an explosion. "Let's get out of here!" yells the sergeant major. "Not onto the platform, the other side!" He pulls the door open and jumps out, and the others follow. Gerhard raises his head and looks towards the open door. He sees the military police running along the tracks. Suddenly the sergeant major appears in the doorway. He aims his pistol at Gerhard's head. Gerhard sees it all happening as if in slow motion. The pale, distorted face of the sergeant major with his finer on the trigger. Gerhard turns his head to the side so as not to see the muzzle flash. He hears the shot and feels a blow. Warm blood runs over his face. He wonders if he's dead, but soon realizes that dead people don't ask questions. His ear hurts, he lies there frozen, not moving a muscle. Minutes pass. Then a voice calls from the platform: "Come out, one by one, with your hands in the air!" Gerhard gets to his feet. "Hands up!" the voice outside calls again. Gerhard turns round and shows his handcuffs. One of the partisans comes in and helps him get out. He is free.

Gerhard tells him that he was to be brought to Paris, where he would probably have been condemned to death and shot. "And none of that happened," says the partisan with the clear voice, whose name is Michel, and who hugs Gerhard. Gerhard feels as if he's in a dream, he looks around in disbelief, into the young faces of the partisans, who laugh as they clap him on the shoulder. A paramedic dabs Gerhard's ear with iodine, it's really just a scratch. If he hadn't twisted his head to the side he'd be dead now. But it's no time for brooding, they've got to hurry because the Germans are probably on their way. Jo, the head of the partisan unit, says there's a smithy opposite the station, where he's sure Gerhard could have his cuffs taken off. The smith, a squat, muscular man, breaks the chain with a blow of his hammer. His daughter, a pretty, dark-haired girl, runs into the house next door and comes back with a big tin of liver pâté. "To make sure you have a quick recovery," she says. He hugs her by way of thanks and bursts into tears.

Gerhard's liberators are members of the Resistance group Francs-Tireurs et Partisans Français, which is run by the Communist Party. "We are all Communists," says a sixteen-year-old who still looks like a child, and whom everyone calls Toutou. They leave Allassac and walk northwards for hours along paths through forests and fields. They

Allassac railway station

stop in an abandoned barn. Now they have time to talk. Gerhard tells them what's happened to him over the past few months, and the others listen excitedly. They decide to accept Gerhard into the partisan army. His code name is "Le Rescapé", the Escapee. He is given an English sub-machine gun, and Michel shows him how to use it. The same day, via his commander, Gerhard applies to become a member of the Communist Party. He is now determined to belong to the people who have saved him, and who are fighting with him against the fascists. This day of liberation must have been like a second birth for Gerhard. The Party will become something like a community of fate to Gerhard, a family that even decades later will be more important to him than anything else. He will devote the rest of his life to it, and no doubt will ever be as strong as the gratitude and joy that he felt that day at the station in Allassac. Others became Communists because they felt drawn to the world of ideas. For Gerhard it's a matter of experience, of feeling, of friendship.

After another three hours on foot they reach the partisan camp. Under cover of the trees there are tents made of red, green and blue parachute silk. There are several fires and field kitchens. There are peasant loaves on linen cloths, mutton with haricot beans is boiling in big pots. About 200 fighters are gathered here. Gerhard sleeps next to a farmer from the Corrèze who has just been given an automatic pistol. He proudly shows his gun and lets the cartridges jump out of the magazine like a cowboy. As he does so a shot goes off, the bullet flies right past Gerhard's head. He has been lucky once again.

12

Victors

TWO DAYS LATER Michel comes charging into Gerhard's tent
early in the morning. He's very agitated. Several times since
five o'clock Radio London has broadcast the coded message that the
Allies have landed in northern France. The message is: "*Dans la forêt
normande il est un lieu-dit.*" (In the Norman forest there is a hamlet.)
Gerhard reflects that the Belgian officer in St Michel prison might have
been right. The battalion commander explains to the fighters that the
offensive of the Resistance groups begins across the whole country. It
is now a matter of interrupting all northbound rail and road connections, and deliberately attacking Wehrmacht bases. Gerhard's unit,
together with other groups, is to attack the *département* capital, Tulle,
where 100 or so heavily armed Wehrmacht soldiers have positioned
themselves in a school building. The partisans drive to the edge of
town in two trucks and a bus. Along with Michel, Gerhard is assigned
to a reconnaissance troop that is to explore the roads. Crouching,
he walks after Michel. What is about to begin is his first real battle.
In his memoirs Gerhard writes: "It took me quite a while to admit
to myself that the feverish excitement that completely takes hold of
me when guns are fired or a skirmish is imminent must actually be
described by the word 'fear'. But I've always tried to reveal nothing

of my agitation. So on that day Michel probably doesn't know how hard it is for me to go with him."

The streets are deserted, and a few hundred metres away salvoes can be heard; clearly the other units have already reached the school. They work their way to the school building, find cover behind a low wall and fire at the windows and doors of the school. Gerhard hears voices from the school building, orders are shouted in German, and then a heavy machine gun starts hammering on the second floor. On Gerhard's right a comrade is hit in the neck, he topples to the floor, bellowing with pain. Gerhard tries to staunch the blood with a cloth, but he can't. Grenades scream into the ground, soil and stones fly through the air. Two men who have been hit fall to the ground behind him. "Let's get out of here!" yells Michel, and the unit retreats.

They don't start again until the following morning. They manage to set the roof of the school alight, the Germans make an escape attempt that ends in a hail of bullets from the partisans, and about forty Wehrmacht soldiers surrender. Gerhard gets his first glimpse of defeated German soldiers. They stand there exhausted, heads lowered, surrounded by partisans at the school entrance. Gerhard translates the words of his commander, who assures the prisoners that nothing will happen to them. "Even though many of us who fell into your hands were murdered." In his memoirs Gerhard writes: "I translate this, and add of my own accord that we are the French People's Army. The Germans don't dare look me in the eye."

What did Gerhard himself feel he was at the time? German? French? He was ten years old when he had to leave Germany, now he's twenty-one. He's grown up in France. He has known the Germans as persecutors, as murderers and sometimes also as saviours. In his notes he sounds deliberately detached when he speaks of "these Teutonic criminals who have spread so much evil across the world". It's as if he wanted to shake off all suspicion that there was any connection between these people and himself. On one occasion a partisan refuses to shake his hand when he finds out that Gerhard is a German. "How can I explain to him that there are also decent people where I come from?" Gerhard wonders. It sounds as if he himself has problems believing it. Before the court martial in Toulouse he had said that he felt like a German with strong connections to the French people. "That's out of the question," the presiding judge had yelled at him. "Anyone who makes a pact with the traditional enemy is no longer a German." Gerhard envies his French comrades, for whom everything is much simpler and clearer. "I would love to hate as they do, but I can't," he notes in Tulle.

In the streets of the town young women are dancing with partisans with sub-machine guns over their shoulders, to the sounds of a *musette* waltz. French flags hang in the windows. The people of Tulle are celebrating the Liberation—a little prematurely, as becomes apparent two hours later, when the sound of heavy gunfire and tank engines is heard. At this point Gerhard's unit has already taken up a position on a slope to the north of the town. From there they can see the tank columns rolling in from the south. Gerhard thinks of the twenty or so wounded partisans lying in the hospital in Tulle along with the wounded German soldiers. A few comrades from Michel's group have commandeered two Gestapo limousines full of explosives, weapons and ammunition. The cars have to be brought to safety as quickly as possible. Gerhard is to drive one of the cars.

Michel says he will drive ahead of him in the other car because he's more familiar with the area. They lose sight of each other on the bendy roads. Just before Perpezac-le-Noir there are women standing in the street waving their arms in the air. Gerhard brakes and throws open the door. One of the women cries, "Lads, turn round. Another car has just crashed into a German tank stopped in the road just around the next bend." Gerhard and his three companions jump from the car, and at that moment a German soldier drives at them on a motorcycle. They fire their sub-machine guns at him and the motorcyclist falls into the ditch. A tank comes round the corner and fires a machine gun at them. Gerhard and the other three flee into the woods. Bullets smash into the branches above their heads. They run until the forest grows denser, and then slump to the ground, exhausted, on a little knoll. Gerhard wonders whether Michel and the others have been able to get away.

They manage to get to the camp. The comrades there already know what's happened. They say Michel and his two companions have been arrested by the SS and taken to Uzerche. An hour later Michel was hanged from a street light before the eyes of the villagers. Gerhard can't listen, he lies down in his tent, shuts his eyes and wants to be a long way away. It's five days since Michel freed him at Allassac station. And now his liberator is dead. If Michel hadn't insisted on driving the first car, Gerhard might be hanging from a street light himself.

Three days later it is revealed that the SS division "Das Reich" had hanged ninety-nine civilians after marching into Tulle, in revenge for the attack by the partisans. The injured comrades in Tulle hospital were killed with shots to the back of the neck the same evening. A couple of days later that same SS division raged through the little town of Oradour-sur Glane, not far from Tulle. Within a few hours 642 men, women and children are murdered. The orders for this crime were issued by SS General Heinz Lammerding, who lived out his life undisturbed in Düsseldorf, and died peacefully in his bed as an affluent businessman in 1971. In France, Lammerding was sentenced to death *in absentia* after the war, and no trial was brought against him in Germany. Only years later Gerhard discovered that it was Lammerding in person who had Michel strung up. The general lived in the house in Uzerche with the street lamp standing outside it. Eyewitnesses later reported that he had watched the partisan's death struggle from the windows of his drawing room.

Once—I must have been about fourteen—I talked to Gerhard about the Wall. I mockingly pointed out that the so-called "anti-fascist protection rampart" had only prevented the citizens of the GDR from getting to the West, but the so-called fascists could cross over to us whenever they wanted. Then Gerhard told me the story of Michel and General Lammerding. In the end Gerhard said he was glad there was a wall to keep criminals like that away from him. I was so shocked by the story that I never again dared talk about the Wall in his presence.

On 16 August the partisans drive back to Tulle. The Wehrmacht garrison has declared itself willing to capitulate. Gerhard stands with his comrades on the bed of a truck. The atmosphere is relaxed, they tell each other funny stories and sing fighting songs. Two weeks previously, Gerhard has been appointed lieutenant, and now leads a group of fighters who have the task of guarding the surrender of a Wehrmacht base. In the afternoon a Wehrmacht envoy reports to the partisans. He suggests taking along a French officer to check the state of the preparations. Gerhard accompanies the envoys and they drive into the forest where the base has been set up. The guards by the gate are startled when they see the partisan with his sub-machine guns. But they let him through. Gerhard thinks for a moment about whether it mightn't be a mistake to come here alone. It could also be a trap, but now it's too late. The head of the base, a colonel, hurries towards him and greets him exuberantly. Gerhard introduces himself as "Lieutenant Rescapé" and the colonel says, "I'm so grateful to the lieutenant for coming so quickly. My warmest thanks again." He even bows. Gerhard doesn't like the man's submissiveness. He knows how the officer would have treated him just a little while ago if he'd got hold of him. The colonel walks ahead of him and points to four gun placements that are still fixed in the ground. "We won't be able to dig these up before the agreed handover, Lieutenant. We need another two hours." Gerhard says those two hours will be granted, but it can't go on any longer than that. "Fine," replies the colonel, clicking his heels.

Gerhard is driven back along the forest path. It all seems so unreal. All of a sudden he is among the victors, and these Germans, who were very much in charge only a few days before, are now saluting him. As if in a time-lapse the pictures race through his head. The prison in Toulouse, the station of Allassac, the tanks in Tulle. He thinks of Michel and the other comrades who didn't have the chance to experience victory. Two hours later the Wehrmacht regiment comes down the path. Six hundred men in rank and file with the colonel at their head. The partisans escort the column on either side. When they arrive in Tulle, the sound of singing reaches them from the centre of town. It is the Marseillaise, sung by hundreds of voices.

13

Toys

I'M SITTING IN THE CAR, driving to see Werner in Berlin-Karow. I'm nervous, far too nervous. I'd actually thought it wouldn't be much of a problem to visit him, because I'm coming not as a grandson but as a genealogist. But it isn't as simple as that. It'll be my second meeting with him. Last time, fourteen years ago, my father was there, and that made things easier. I was the observer of a reunion. Now I'm meeting my grandfather. That sounds normal. But what do I know about this man? What does he know about me? On the phone I have to explain to him who I even am. He had forgotten my name. "I'm Wolf's eldest son," I said. Then there was silence for a few seconds. I heard him breathing. "Ah, Wolf's son. Then come by," he said.

Werner comes to meet me on the stairs. He has thick, white hair and eyes that lie deep in their sockets. He's ninety-five years old now, but when he smiles he looks younger. Werner smiles a lot. I tell him I want to write a book, and I'd like to ask him a few questions about his life. He doesn't hear very well, and I have to say it twice. Werner leads me unsteadily to a glass case in the living room, which contains a faded yellow ID. The passport photograph, stamped with a swastika eagle, shows a serious-looking boy with a shaved hairline and a

Werner's identification papers for the 1936 Olympics

pomaded quiff. It's Werner's identification papers as a participant in the 1936 Olympic Games. "That was the most lovely time," says Werner. "Lovelier than anything else." Werner took part in the opening ceremony. He performed with thousands of other gymnasts on the pitch of the Olympic Stadium in Berlin. He has a photograph of that performance, taken from the back row of the stadium. The athletes can only be made out as tiny white dots. They form a huge cross and five Olympic rings. I don't know what the cross means, whether it turned into a swastika in the course of the performance. But I can imagine how well Werner, that tall, dark-blond adolescent with the grey-blue eyes, fitted in with that spectacle. We try to talk a little, and I ask him how he met my grandmother Sigrid. Werner thinks for a moment, closes his eyes, and his jaw works back and forth. He tries to concentrate, to settle on a memory. But then there's nothing more. Eventually he gives up, opens his eyes and shrugs with embarrassment. It seems I've come too late.

Werner gets photograph albums out of a cupboard. Perhaps that will bring the memories back. The black-and-white photographs are neatly mounted and captioned. Skiing holiday in the Tyrolean Alps in 1938, Werner on a sun-lounger. His training with an anti-aircraft unit in Lankwitz in 1939, Werner proud and bolt upright in his corporal's uniform. Fresh air on the Wannsee in the summer of 1936, Werner and Sigrid cuddling in their wicker beach chair. "My summer holiday" is written in German script in the margin. Bürgerpark, Pankow, 1940, Werner laughing in his army coat in the snow. Whitsun 1937 in the Müggelberge, Werner playing handball with members of his gymnastics club. In these photograph albums the so-called "Third Reich" looks like a cheerful dream holiday.

I feel myself becoming uneasy. There's none of what I associate with those years. Those laughing faces, that carefree attitude, it all baffles me. I can't help thinking of Gerhard, who was on the run at the time. Werner smiles dreamily, lost now in those pictures of his youth. "It was lovely," he murmurs, running his fingers over the yellowing photographs. I don't dare ask him my questions. I tell myself that he probably wouldn't understand them anyway. I tell myself that everyone tries to transform his youth, however disagreeable the circumstances really were. So Werner was a long way from being a Nazi. But the idea doesn't really reassure me. He throws my whole image of the family into disarray. It was clear to me that I came from a Jewish Resistance family, and now Werner turns up and shows me how great things were under the Nazis. Everything within me rebels at the idea of getting close to this man. Of accepting that he belongs to my family. That I belong to his family.

Still, I take a closer look at the pictures. The resemblance between him and me is striking. He has the same thin legs, the same slightly bent posture, the same nose, the same mouth, the same profile. Now I understand why Grandma Sigrid always said I was like her "Wernerle" long ago. There is a photograph in which Werner lies on his side outside a tent, supporting himself on his left elbow and eating. That's exactly how I've often seen my father eat, and exactly how I lie when we're having a picnic. I can't simply reject this man. He's too close to me. I want to know who he is.

Above all I want to know if Werner was a Nazi. He takes a few boxes of papers out of a cupboard. Werner has carefully saved and filed everything. That at least. I find a CV that he wrote in the Fifties when he was applying to join the SED. He writes that his political attitude in the Third Reich was "vague and emotional". "My father's political outlook inclined towards National Socialism at the time. In conversations he would instil great doubts and conflicts in me. I always refused all exhortations to take part in demonstrations. I adopted a critical wait-and-see attitude." In another file is Werner's *Ahnenpass*, his "proof of ancestry" from the register office and the church archive, in which it is attested that he "has been of Aryan blood for at least three generations". Werner gives me a book covered in grey linen. He himself has printed and bound it. It's his life story, which he recorded "for posterity" at the end of the Eighties. Werner's vanity is my good fortune.

Later, at home, I start reading. Werner describes his childhood in Göritz, a village in Uckermark, where he grew up on his grandparents' farm. His father, a builder, was at war, and his mother, who worked as a salesgirl before she got married, didn't have the money to stay with the boy in Berlin. His grandfather has two horses, two cows, three pigs, a few chickens and lots of geese. Four-year-old Werner's job is to look after them. Every day and in all kinds of weather he takes the geese to the meadow to feed. Sometimes they fly away from him, and then he has to run after them and catch them again. He's so tired in the evening that he often goes to sleep over dinner. His grandfather is a large man with bushy eyebrows. A former policeman, now a clerk and registrar in the village. Sometimes Werner creeps into the register office at weddings, stands beside the door behind a filing cabinet and doesn't make a sound. It strikes Werner that the bride is always much younger than the groom. His grandfather later explains to him that the farmers seek out the daughters of other farmers, mostly so that their fields fit together. These weddings aren't particularly cheerful affairs. Everyone looks very serious, and when the wedding is over the groom takes a hip flask out of his pocket and all the men are allowed to take a good swig.

When the weather is good, Werner goes swimming with the other village children in the pond beside the fire station. Before they go swimming they throw three dead frogs in the water to appease the pond spirit who likes to drag children into the depths, or so say the adults, who see water as a dangerous business. When his grandmother catches him swimming, he gets an earful. At Christmas his father takes a holiday from the war, because there is no fighting on feast days, which strikes Werner as eminently sensible. His father is a Zieten Hussar, he wears a field-grey uniform with gold cords dangling from it, and black riding boots with five-pointed spurs that you can spin. Werner writes that he didn't know very much about his father. Nor, in all likelihood, did his father about him. His father has a pale, narrow face and a moustache from which little icicles hang in the winter. He doesn't say much, and his eyes gaze wearily past Werner. His father is happiest when tending to the horses, and with his brother he drinks brandy that he's brought from France. After Christmas he rides back to battle.

When the First World War is over, Werner moves to Berlin with his parents. They have a little flat in the working-class district of Wedding. There is a sitting room, a kitchen and a dining room. The city seems so big and inhospitable that he soon becomes homesick. He misses the meadows and the wide sky, the village pond and grandfather's parlour. His father works in a power station, and goes to the pub after work, often coming home very late at night. On Sunday his father lies on the sofa and reads the paper or sleeps. Then Werner has to be quiet, because his father gets angry when anybody wakes him up. On the other hand his mother is there for him, and he can talk to her about anything. She makes him something to eat when he comes home from school. There is salted herring with potatoes boiled in their skins, or vegetables with bacon sauce. After his snack Werner does his homework, and then he's allowed back into the street and doesn't have to come back until the gaslights are lit outside. Later they sit down to dinner at the kitchen table and Werner asks if Papa is coming home today. And his mother's eyes are sad, and eventually Werner stops asking.

It is very different when his father is on his summer holiday. Then he is always at home, because he doesn't meet his colleagues and go drinking beer with them. During these weeks his father makes precise miniature horse ploughs, coaches and farmhouses that Werner is then allowed to play with. The toys are in Werner's siting-room display cabinet, arranged around his Olympic papers. There is a little yellow post cart, a bronze dray and a fire engine assembled from tiny strips of wood. Next to that is a stable with a hoist for lifting tiny bags of straw, and an inn with a brown wooden veranda. I'd heard about these things, because Wolf had told me about them. When he was little, Werner also let him play with them. Wolf says the toys were only used by children who didn't have a real father.

At fourteen Werner becomes a member of a gymnastics club, and also begins to draw. Twice a week he goes to evening classes at the College of Art on Grunewaldstrasse. There is also a life drawing class there. Werner is terribly excited the first time he goes. He's never seen a naked woman before, and he's disappointed. The woman, standing floodlit on a plinth in the studio, has flabby, drooping breasts, varicose veins and lank hair. Werner draws her as he would like to see her. It's a pretty picture, but the course leader isn't pleased. "Here we draw women as they are," he says, and Werner has to start all over again. Werner has talent: the professor advises him to stick at it, and maybe even take a course of study at the college. When Werner tells his father, his father laughs at him. He tells him to learn a decent craft like everyone else in the family. "Studying art isn't for people like us," his father says. And that's the end of it. At sixteen Werner takes an apprenticeship as a model-builder in a foundry, because his father knows the boss of a model factory. In the meantime the global economic crisis is spreading, and unemployment is on the rise. Werner should be glad that he has the chance to learn anything at all. Work in the factory is hard. Werner has to carry wood, sweep the factory floor and carry huge bags of glue. Twice a week he has to deliver the finished models to the customers in big baskets. If he does anything wrong, he is yelled at by the boss or punched in the stomach by the other apprentices.

There are lots of demonstrations in the streets. "Class against class", it says on the Communists' posters. Werner doesn't know what it means. He thinks it might have something to do with school. At home in Wedding, the Communists engage in street battles with the National Socialists. People are beaten up or even killed. At the Kristallpalast cinema they show the anti-war film *All Quiet on the Western Front*. The Nazis riot and throw bottles of ink at the screen. The Nazi thugs scare Werner. Most people have been made redundant at the foundry. Only the foreman toils away with six apprentices in the production hall. Just before Werner's apprenticeship certification exam his father dies of tuberculosis. On his last visit to the hospital his father gives him a silver Thaler. A memento.

Along with his certificate, Werner receives his release papers. In one of the files I find a letter from the factory owner, Alwin Schrumpf, testifying that Werner has been fired "only on grounds of lack of work". The letter is dated 3 March 1933. Werner is nineteen. From now on he goes twice a week to the dole office on Gormannstrasse, where he is given one mark eighty-seven pfennigs. One mark fifty of this goes to his mother in expenses. Of the few pfennigs left over he can't even afford a tram journey. That is how his adult life begins. The queue outside the dole office on Gormannstrasse gets longer every week. A man he knows there advises him to go to the "Brown House" on the Lützowufer. "They're always looking for people."

Werner goes there and asks. They need part-time workers for the railways, but you only get a job if you become a member of the SA. These are the thugs that Werner has encountered before, so he opts instead to keep going to the dole office.

After a few months the situation in Germany changes. "However much the workers might curse Hitler, he creates work," Werner notes. "Many people's views and political opinions are changing." Whether his own views are changing, he doesn't say. But now he can work for weeks at a time in the model factory again, and from 1935 he is even taken on full-time. He receives "a very decent wage", which is also urgently needed, because by now his mother has used up all her savings and her widow's pension isn't even enough to keep her alive, let alone her and her son. Now Werner is the breadwinner, and that makes him proud. "At last I can take charge of my own life, all of a sudden everything seems possible," he writes. A few months before at the gymnastics club he met Sigrid, who is five years younger than he, almost a child. They spend every free minute together. They go out, dance the tango, the waltz and the slow foxtrot in cafés in the park. They even win prizes, they're such a handsome couple. There are lots of photographs of her in Werner's albums. "Sigrid doing gymnastics 1936", it says on one page. She is sitting on the barre, her head tilted towards the sky and her legs outstretched. It could be one of those propaganda photographs showing the new, Germanic person. And they were just practising sport. But even that strikes me as suspect. The two of them seem too comfortable with the times, with the years of the body cult and the pomaded quiff. It all hangs together too neatly for me, the proud, blue-eyed workers' children and the cries of *"Sieg Heil"*. I grew up with those truths. For me there was nothing innocent, nothing normal about Germany in 1936. Anyone normal belonged to the other side.

I visit Sigrid. She's now living in an old people's home run by the workers' welfare organization, in Hohenschönhausen. Visiting her is fun, because she's always so delighted. I owe Grandma Sigrid my first serious experience with alcohol. When I was fourteen, I emptied half a bottle of advocaat with her in the campsite. She only ever talked about the war, and I couldn't get a word in. When I was a child she was my favourite grandma, because she let me watch television until closedown at her house, and eat cheesecake till I was sick. I could do what I liked, she always thought I was great, because I was like her Wernerle. Sigrid still clearly remembers her first few years with Werner. The boat trips on Lake Tegel, the skiing holidays in Carinthia, the cycling trips to Birkenwerder and the visits to the cinema on the Kurfürstendamm. She worked as a shorthand typist in the Raddatz & Co. department store on Leipziger Strasse. They went on outings with the gymnastics club and did amateur theatricals. Sigrid's eyes gleam when she talks about those times. "All the confusion was over, my mother cooked very nicely, and I had Werner. They were the happiest years of my life."

The only nuisance, says Sigrid, was the constant political discussions. If Werner was convinced about something, he always had to convince everybody else as well. Werner was very keen on National Socialism, he had raved about the new age, about new possibilities. "He liked order, he liked punctuality." And at last he had work again. "Nazism is posh Communism," he used to say. Sigrid didn't really understand what he meant, and she didn't ask because she was much happier dancing with Werner than talking to him about politics. But Werner had argued with her father Fritz, she says. He banged on at him evening after evening, but Fritz, who was more inclined to sympathize with the Communists, wouldn't be convinced.

Wolf even says that the arguments once got so violent that Werner threatened to inform on his father-in-law for anti-government propaganda. Werner actually ran to the police station, but it was already shut. The next day his fury had vanished, so Fritz was free from the threat of denunciation.

Sigrid can't remember this affair. It strikes her as a bit of an exaggeration. On the other hand, she says, she does like to remember the nice things. Wolf says the story of the denunciation happened exactly as described. Fritz had told him everything, and Fritz hadn't been inclined to exaggerate. I don't know what I'm supposed to believe. Can you forget that the man you've loved wanted to throw your own father to the lions? Or did Sigrid forget it because she wouldn't have been able to live with Werner? If that's true, what would have happened to Fritz if the police station had in fact been open?

Sigrid talks about an argument with Werner after their marriage, when they had found their first flat, a room in Pankow. Werner was determined to put a swastika flag in the window. Sigrid thought that was stupid, she didn't want banners all over the place, not least because of her father. In the end they agreed just to buy a very small flag, but then Werner came back with the biggest flag he could find. Apparently the small ones were sold out. He put up flagpoles on the balcony of his parents-in-law's apartment too. He would even have supplied the flags, Sigrid says, but Fritz forbade him from putting up the Nazi flags. Twenty years later Werner bought red flags for Fritz's balcony. But that was quite a different story.

14

Jottings

NONE OF THIS MAKES IT SOUND as if Werner really had such a "critical wait-and-see attitude" as he claimed in his CV in the Fifties. It sounds more as if he, like many others, had been convinced by the idea of the better life. He noticed that things were moving forwards, that his life was getting nicer, and that even the children of workers suddenly had a chance. No one in his family had ever been skiing in the mountains before. He was also the first to see the sea. Even if they'd had the money, it would never have occurred to his parents to hire a wicker deckchair or buy a bottle of wine at a tea dance at the Wannsee. Werner felt like a social climber, like someone who'd struck lucky. "All of a sudden anything seems possible," he writes, and that was probably the feeling that many people had in those days. Hitler made the little people big and the big people small. Gerhard, the son of the *haute bourgeoisie*, had to leave the country, while worker's son Werner was able to enjoy the high life.

When Werner writes his memoirs in the Eighties, the process of repression has plainly advanced still further. He writes: "When the

Third Reich was imposing its violent rule on every level, I was gloomy about this brutal form of government, and went on trying to find a solution for myself. If I didn't salute the Nazi flag, didn't go to any Nazi rallies and didn't want to pay the contribution to the 'German Labour Front' in advance, I got into trouble. I scratched out the little swastika in the bronze medal I received for taking part in the Olympic Games. But even that didn't change anything. I practised passive resistance, without supporting any counter-actions." All of this is probably true. Werner isn't the kind of person who makes things up. But he's also very good at forgetting awkward things. It's possible that in 1936 he really did scratch out the swastika from his Olympic medal, and in 1941 he was absolutely required to have quite a large swastika flag in his first flat. That he was hesitant at first, and eventually enthusiastic. Sigrid says that in the winter of 1942 he voluntarily gave his skis and warm underwear for the soldiers in Russia. "His skis were the holiest of holies as far as he was concerned, and he himself could have used the underwear. But he said everybody must do his bit for the final victory."

I asked Sigrid what she'd known at the time about the crimes of the Nazis. She had to think a little. "We didn't worry about them," she said. She'd remembered a few things. There was a girl in the neighbourhood with curly blonde hair, called Nina Haller. Eventually the girl disappeared, because she was a Jew. Her Jewish headmistress, who had always ensured that children from poor families, like Sigrid, got *Wurstbrote* from the richer families, suddenly wasn't there either. "But that was just how things were, we didn't ask any questions, perhaps we were scared," says Sigrid.

In February 1941 she goes on honeymoon with Werner to Hohnstein in "Saxon Switzerland", the hills south-east of Dresden. There is a fortress on a mountain. People say locally that it's a concentration camp. Sigrid says that one night trucks full of prisoners drove through Hohnstein. But that can't be true, because Hohnstein concentration camp was closed down in 1934. Perhaps the people there told her about the transports. At any rate Sigrid says that none of it really touched her. After all, they were on honeymoon. "I thought we had the right to a bit of fun. Later on, everything got difficult enough."

Werner didn't have to go to war for some time yet. The model factory where he works supplies components for arms manufacturing. He is categorized as "deferred from military service" and is allowed to stay in Berlin. Wolf is born in 1942. Because of the increasing air raids on Berlin, in summer 1943 he sends Sigrid and the baby to stay with a cousin who lives in a village in Saxony. He himself receives a cure in the Baltic spa town of Kühlungsborn in recognition of his major contribution to the war effort. On the train journey there he meets a woman called Lilly, with whom he will spend this holiday. A year later Lilly falls pregnant with his child. On 9 September Werner has to report to the Hindenburg barracks in Bremen. He is trained to fire an anti-aircraft gun, and at the end of September he goes with his unit to the Lüneberg Heath, where he is to take part in manoeuvres. Werner sees the red and gold heather and the brown and green forests. He thinks it's a shame "that we have to wreck this dreamlike landscape with our grenades, and disturb the later summer calm". He clearly hasn't heard much about the war that's been raging for five years in Europe.

In mid-December 1944 the regiment is assembled in Nettlingen. They are to halt the advancing American tanks in the Alsatian Ardennes. It's the Wehrmacht's last act of defiance on the Western Front. Werner probably doesn't know at the time how pointless it is. It's part of the last gasp. Werner kept a diary about his time in the

Werner and Sigrid on their wedding day, 1941

war, in which he recorded in great detail everything that happened during his absence from home. I found the diary on a bookshelf in his flat, beside a first edition of the constitution of the GDR. Werner was amazed when I showed him the battered black notebook. He had already forgotten about it. The pages are closely written. Werner has beautiful, neat handwriting. Even the first lines, which he wrote in a hole in the ground in Alsace, seem concentrated and orderly. The hole is his dugout, two metres deep, frozen earth, three metres away from his grenade launcher. A blizzard is raging. It's 31 December 1944. "When we fire the regimental salvo it's five minutes to midnight. The grenades take with them my best wishes for the Yanks. The whole horizon is bright when the grenades land over there. Amazing New Year's fireworks display. Boy, I wouldn't fancy being a Yank. Two hundred and seventy shots, that's 670 hundredweight of steel and explosive whizzing over there. By the time we've reloaded and aimed at the new target, it's two minutes after midnight. So it's 1945. I think about home for a minute. Are they still awake? I don't think so. I'm sure Mutti is asleep, and so is Sigrid unless there's a raid. They give us tablets here so that we don't go to sleep. I can hardly feel my fingers, it's so bloody cold."

The next morning, just after dawn, American fighter bombers fly over. "They don't dare touch us, they're scared of our anti-aircraft fire, they're Americans, after all. German fighter pilots would have done everything quite differently." Werner sounds as if he's been there for months. His soldierly first-person-plural is routine by now, and he doesn't seem to have any doubts about his mission. A few pages later, on the other hand, he writes with horror: "The Yank is shooting at our gun emplacements. We've had our first fatality. Our radio operator got a grenade splinter in his head. After about ten seconds he was dead. I have a funny feeling in my stomach when he's laid on the truck. His name was Mehrling, and he played the piano beautifully on our farewell evening in Nettlingen. It's such a tiny step from life to death."

Werner has barely slept for five days. He repeatedly dozes off even when he's walking, he falls on his face in the snow and gets up again, startled. He's wearing two shirts, two pairs of underpants, two pullovers, a drill suit, a mortar suit and a coat. He's still cold. On 5 January it occurs to him that his daughter Rita is now a year old. "In the dark hole in the ground, Franz is already asleep, I think about home and about Rita. I cry a bit and go to sleep."

Over the months that follow a hasty retreat begins. Werner has recorded the dates and places in tiny handwriting on a sheet of A4 paper: "13.3. Niederbronn, buried Pawelczek (…) 21.3. Kaplanai-Hof, 15 minutes' barrage against our position (armour-piercing shells) (…) 24–26.3. Friedrichstal, 1st bath since Hildesheim." In spite of his hunger and his constant terror he does seem to have some romantic dalliances during this time, which he records in brief notes: "1–3.4. Hohenklingen (young farmer's daughter, about twenty-four, father and brother fallen, mother dead, would have liked to keep me, twenty-five acres of land! She wanted to give me civilian clothes). I was scared, the SS was after us (…) 9–16.4. Rienharz, with a Rhineland girl, jolly evenings (…) 20–23.4. Schwörsheim, as a private lodger in the flat of a young war widow, Elsa Taglieber."

The next detailed entry is dated 1 May 1945, 2 p.m., Westendorf. Werner writes in pencil: "We arrive here at nine o'clock with our mortar division. At twelve the Yank fires into the village. We have recognized the pointlessness of fighting on, and decide to accept that we'll be taken prisoner. Our officers drive on into the Alps. We tip the mortars down a hill, bury the aiming equipment and the optical devices. The Yank is 700 metres behind us on the motorway, and doesn't dare come in to get us. We still have enough food and time. I sit in a parlour, reading and thinking. It's actually a shame that it's all going to be over today or tomorrow. I'd have liked to go on running until the war was over so that I could get home without being taken prisoner. But I've had it up to here with being chased every day, and with the lack of ammunition. We play forfeit games with a farmer's daughter and another young woman till midnight, then we lie down on the floor to sleep. The next day a Pole comes at eleven and says the Yanks are telling us to hand ourselves over. We march in march formation to the Yanks. The first sentry tells us to throw our guns on a pile. A little further along, a Yank addresses us in German. He looks like a drunken cowboy. He wears dark glasses around his helmet, and a coloured scarf around his neck. In each hand he holds a pistol. So the war is over for me."

They spend a few nights crammed together in a barn, on 6 May the prisoners are taken via Munich and Augsburg to Heilbronn. They sit in a field surrounded by a barbed-wire fence. There are heavy machine guns at the four corners of the fence. It's hot and there's no water, at midday a few buckets of rust-brown broth are passed over the fence, but by now there are at least 20,000 people in the camp, Werner guesses. He lies on the hard mud floor and tries to sleep. Time passes, it's unbearably hot by day and at night the temperature falls below zero. No one knows how long they will have to stay here, or what's going to happen to them. The surrounding fields are also being fenced off, and new prisoner transports are arriving every day. There's hardly anything to eat, and even water is in short supply. Werner tries not to move too quickly, because it makes him dizzy. The first men collapse and are taken away, others go completely mad and can only be calmed with great difficulty. Werner records: "Here you see everyone as he really is, lots of people lose their composure. They push their way to the water tap like animals, no one wants to wait. I'm avoiding any pointless movement. Saving strength. Anyone who falls and doesn't get up is lost."

A week later they are divided according to postcode and assigned new places in the camps. Werner hopes that the process of their release will begin soon. On 21 July they march to Heilbronn freight station, accompanied by American soldiers with sub-machine guns at the ready. They climb aboard freight trains, thirty men per carriage. A railwayman whispers to them that the train is bound for France. "We're stunned, the little bit of strength we derived from the hope of an imminent return home has fled all of a sudden. I feel profound despair. I don't even have the strength to cry." They travel via Strasbourg and Nancy to Le Mans in eastern France. There they end up once again in a camp in an open field. It is forbidden to get closer than five metres to the barbed-wire fence. An over-zealous prisoner assigned to cleaning duties goes closer to the fence to pick up a piece of paper. The sentry fires at him and the man roars with pain. A paramedic is called. He comes and kneels down by the injured man. The sentry also shoots at the paramedic, who dies immediately. Werner watches all this without any particular emotion. "I'm too weak to be really sad. I forget the names of my comrades, even trying to do small sums creates difficulties." There is a small photograph in one of Werner's albums that was taken at this time. At first glance you wouldn't recognize him. Werner is emaciated, has a full beard and long hair. His gaze is dull.

At this time his diary is his closest companion. He has smuggled it through all the checks, in a double-bottomed suitcase. After being taken prisoner by the Americans he writes: "For all my misfortune, I have been lucky after all. My pen and notebook are there." The diary is his friend, in whom he can confide everything. During the first few weeks in France his handwriting is unsteady and indistinct. That is probably due in part to the exhaustion he writes about. On 22 August he notes: "It takes a lot of self-control to continue with this diary. But it's the only meaningful thing remaining to me." He describes in great detail life in the camp, the food portions, the weather, his comrades. About the lost war, about the Third Reich that has just collapsed, he doesn't waste a word. Is he perhaps afraid that his diary might one day fall into the hands of his guards? Or is this not the time for political reflections? By day Werner now digs mass graves. He gets double rations for that, and feels his strength slowly returning. In the morning they throw the corpses of comrades who have died in the night into the graves. Twenty corpses per grave. Then they pour on lime and soil, because otherwise it begins to stink after a few days. In the sick barracks Werner sees comrades he remembers from Heilbronn. "They have tuberculosis, and are not to be saved. I will bury them all, that much is certain. At the same time my fear of becoming ill myself is growing. This is a death sentence."

I have compared the dates and established that Werner arrived in France just before Gerhard left his French exile for Germany. For Gerhard the time of uncertainty is coming to an end, for Werner it's just beginning. I try to imagine what it would have been like if the two of them had met at this time. The victorious French lieutenant and the captured German corporal. Gerhard dealt with German prisoners of war a lot, he even visited the camps to tell Wehrmacht soldiers of the crimes of the Nazis. When Werner arrives in Le Mans, Gerhard has just turned up in Paris, and sees his father again for the first time since the end of the war. France has become both men's destiny, but in very different ways.

15

Pains

WERNER IS LUCKY, AS EVER. In early April 1946 he ends up in a group of prisoners distributed around the surrounding farms. One farmer, by the name of Jean, seeks him out because he's the tallest man in the group. He asks him what he does for a living and Werner says "farmer". Only a few days later, when it becomes clear that he has no idea about ploughing, harrowing or milking, Werner admits that he's actually a model-maker. He's allowed to stay on anyway, because he's a quick learner and a hard worker. "A lot of work, a lot of food," the farmer told him on the first day. The day begins at five o'clock. First Werner cleans out the stables, then he milks the cows and works in the garden. In the afternoon he goes out into the field. Work stops at half past seven. The food is abundant and delicious. "For the first time in ages I'm able to eat as much as I like. Communication with the boss is primitive but successful. Grabbing my bottom and saying 'boom, boom, boom' means peas. Today the boss weighed me, eighty-two kilos. The days consist only of eating, working and sleeping. In bed I still play the mouth organ and think about mother, Sigrid and the children."

The work is hard. Werner has blisters on his hands and can barely move his right knee. He trudges behind the oxen pulling the plough, in wooden clogs. The seed rows seem incredibly long to him. He notices himself getting dull, his brain closing down and all of his life going into his body. He recites poems out loud and delivers little lectures about electricity and technical drawing. He wonders if a brain gets smaller if it isn't used. On 21 April Werner writes: "Last night when I went to bed it occurred to me that it was the Führer's birthday." Is it possible that he doesn't know that Hitler's been dead for almost a year? Does he know anything at all about the world beyond the French farm? Has he had news of his family? Werner describes everyday life in obsessive detail, but there are no thoughts about anything beyond the everyday. There is a photograph showing him and Jean the farmer. Werner is wearing a tie under his jacket, and is more than a head taller than the Frenchman. The farmer is a squat little chap. In the photograph Werner looks like the boss. Clearly that's also the opinion of the madame of the house, as Werner calls her. More and more often the two of them stay up together in the parlour long after everyone else has gone to bed. "The *patron* is grumpy, he's as attentive as a shooting dog."

They're now working from dawn till dusk. At lunchtime there's a break for an hour because the draught animals need a rest. Werner has pains in the small of his back and cracks in his hands, and his left wrist is swollen. "I don't know if my arse is still attached to my pelvis or whether it's hanging from a string." Sunday is the day of rest. Werner thinks of Lilly, his holiday romance, who has just turned twenty-six. He describes how they met back on the train to Kühlungsborn. They sat facing one another in the compartment, and he couldn't take his eyes off her. They fell into conversation, and when they arrived at the Baltic they had told each other their most intimate thoughts. Lilly got out in Kühlungsborn Ost, and he had to travel on. They arranged to meet at the beach and spent every day and soon every night together. "I'm happy, I feel as if I've met the woman of my life," Werner writes. Then there are two crossed-out passages in the diary, the only passages he's deleted, the ones no one else is supposed to read. After the blacked-out passages he writes about the child born after that holiday. "Very few people would forgive me for bringing this child into the world, but they wouldn't reproach me for taking the lives of hundreds of people in the war with my gun. What sort of strange morality is that? What sort of times are these? As far as possible, I will give my little Heinz the feeling that he has a father, even if his father isn't with him. It would be nice if Sigrid and Wolf were here now. I'm hopelessly alone again."

On 30 May 1946 Werner gets his first letter from Sigrid. A year after the start of his imprisonment. All that time he plainly didn't know what was happening to his family. Sigrid writes that everyone is well. She encloses photographs of Wolf and Rita. Werner is proud of his son because he looks so much like him. He is beside himself with joy, and replies that now that fate has been kind to him he is ready "to be a decent family man who will, I hope, no longer stray from the right path". It's a kind of oath of loyalty, a statement of faith. "I want to climb the ladder of my ability right to the top. Where my ability stops, I will put my boy. I will make sure that he doesn't have to start his ascent right at the bottom as I did. He won't start his life with just a primary-school education. Soon I will tell him all that I am and all that I can do."

It will be another year and a half before Werner can finally set off for home. A year and a half in which he slogs away on the farm, day in and day out, and has no idea when his imprisonment will be over. I don't know what happens to him during this time, his notes become increasingly irregular. He hardly gives away any of his thoughts and feelings. Some days he just records his weight, his pulse and the state of his digestion.

On 30 September 1947 he becomes a little more forthcoming again. On that day he boards a train with thirty other prisoners in Le Mans. They are heading back to Germany. "I've been waiting for this moment for all those years, and now the time has come, and I'm a bit confused because everything's going to be different from now on. I almost think I've got used to being a prisoner and don't know where it goes from here." They travel via Saarbrücken, Mannheim, Frankfurt, Hanau and Bebra to Eisenach, where they arrive late on the evening of 10 October. They are registered, examined and deloused. He is granted permission to send a telegram to his family in Berlin. Among Werner's papers I find the registration form for Eisenach transit camp. "Well fed, normal responsiveness, no vermin detected," it says on the form. They pass through three other camps before he is finally able to board the train to Berlin.

"We arrive in Berlin at six o'clock in the morning on 28.10. That is the big moment for which we've been waiting for years. I want to absorb this last piece of homeward journey whole, and enjoy it with a clear consciousness. When I step out of Gesundbrunnen U-Bahn station, I have the feeling of being really at home for the first time. In a few minutes I'll be at my place, and how will that be? I still have my key to the apartment. I quietly open the kitchen door and go in. The kitchen is smaller than I remember it. On the kitchen table there is a bunch of flowers with a welcome message, it looks as if they've been expecting me. I prepare myself for the first greeting, wash myself, comb my hair and brush my teeth, I'm calm but slightly agitated. Sigrid calls, who's there? It's the same voice as before. What am I supposed to say? I don't say anything. I hear footsteps, the door opens. When I pull away from Sigrid's first embrace I see Wolf and Rita. Both, and Sigrid too, look just like their pictures in my memory."

Here the diary stops. It is only four months later, on 24 March 1948, that Werner writes again. It is his last entry: "Time has passed quickly, and much has happened and changed. After I greeted my loved ones again, my imprisonment vanished like a dream. Life picks up at the precise point when I received my call-up notice. At home, everything is fine, by and large. I'm pleased with the boy. He's turning out just as I'd imagined and hoped. But the girl hasn't had the upbringing that her character needs. I want to have a determining effect on her, to achieve her acknowledgement of me. I think I have found the way, which will also force Sigrid to be rather tougher with her. After a few violent discussions between Sigrid and me about her management of the household and her domestic duties, she is trying to fulfil my wishes. I myself have lost a lot of weight lately, I'm constantly shivering, and filled with internal unease. I've just had lunch, and now I'm looking out of the window, calmly for the first time. The cobbles in the street drift past the houses like a strip of stone. How heavy must it weigh on the earth below? I feel as if all the cobblestones are weighing down on me."

It just can't go on like that. How could it, after everything Werner has been through? I don't know whether he was able to talk to Sigrid about it. About the horrors in the war and in the camps, about his fears, his loneliness. Did they have time for such conversations? Or was the hardship in the winter of 1948 still so great, even at home, that there was no time to worry about past hardships? Perhaps Werner didn't want to talk, he just wanted to forget it all as quickly as possible.

It would be in keeping with his character if he had wanted to sort it all out on his own. If he suffered in silence under the pressure of memory. And then sometimes lost his temper, hit his son, yelled at his wife. The pressure had to go somewhere. It's easy to condemn him today, to present him as an angry father and a bad husband. But it's possible that Werner couldn't have acted otherwise, that the years abroad had blunted him. If you're in constant danger, if your sole concern is to save your own skin, if you spend months lying in the dirt, watching your comrades die, can you be normal again straight away? Can you ever be normal again?

Werner tries, he won't leave himself in peace, it's almost as if peace is what he fears. A dreamy glance out of the window will have to do. As long as Werner is functioning, as long as he is being active, he can keep the past at arm's length.

Three weeks after his return he goes to the labour exchange, where he says he wants to be either a teacher in a vocational school or a stage-set painter. They give him the addresses of the main school authority and the stage workshops. Werner stands at the tram stop and can't make up his mind. He decides to get onto the first tram that comes along. It rattles and squeaks along to the school authority building on the Werdersche Markt, past burnt-out ruins. Werner sees for the first time the ruined state of the centre of Berlin. The school authority, a formerly magnificent building, looks uninhabitable from the outside. Inside, Werner gets lost in the passageways and corridors that end in bricked-up doors. He climbs creaking stairs, with rats darting around beneath them. Werner wonders what the schools must look like if the administration is in such a state. An elderly gentleman shows him the way to the personnel department. There he is welcomed with open arms. Teachers are urgently needed. Only two days later he sits the exam for teacher-training college.

I'm surprised that Werner allowed his professional future to be determined by a tram. The stage workshops were in Kreuzberg at the time. If the other tram had come first, Werner would have remained a West Berliner, my parents would never have met, and I would never have been born.

At any rate, Werner passes the teacher-training entrance exam. He is allowed to join the current semester, and becomes a teaching assistant in a vocational school for carpenters in the furniture and building trades. Werner goes home, completely taken aback because everything's going so quickly. A month after his return he has jumped into a new life.

At the end of 1947 there are different sectors in Berlin, but it still doesn't really matter where you live or work. The administrative offices and colleges, if they haven't been bombed to smithereens, are where they were before the war. The main school authority happens to be in the Russian zone, as is the teacher-training college. So Werner isn't making a political decision when he decides to study in the East. Anyone who wants to be a teacher at this time has to go there. The political division of Berlin isn't completed until October 1948. From that point onwards the administrations in East and West Berlin are separate. At teacher-training college Werner finds new support, largely thanks to Heinz Wenzel, whom he meets there. Wenzel is a bit older than Werner, and works as a lecturer at the college. Werner is impressed with him because he knows so much and has a sensible-sounding answer to almost every question. "At a time when so few people have perspective, it's nice to meet someone who does," Werner writes on a birthday card to Wenzel. Werner is trying to find his bearings, to find which direction to take. And Wenzel is looking for people like Werner, for people who are malleable and ready for the new future. Wenzel is a Communist, a member of the KPD since 1927. In the Third Reich he disappeared and lived in hiding, and wrote school books "for the time to come". To do that you did need perspective. And optimism.

At home Werner only ever talks about Heinz. He too wants to be a Communist now, and starts reading Marx and Engels. As always with Werner it all happens very quickly. And this time, once again, he can't keep his enthusiasm to himself. Everybody has to join in, everybody has to listen when Werner comes out with his new truths. Two weeks after the start of his work as a teaching assistant, Werner writes his first report for the headmaster's office. Among the chief difficulties of his work he mentions "impressions of the world of ideas from the Nazi era which persist in the pupils". It is necessary "to make these young students understand the reason for the German defeat, explain the concept of democracy and also practise it in school". In this respect the teacher must be a model. When I read this I'm flummoxed. What's happened to his own Nazi world of ideas? Did it just disappear like that? Does he now believe that it never existed? Or with his directives, is he referring not to the pupils, but to himself?

While Werner is studying, the GDR is established, a new struggle begins, and now his decision to remain in the East is partly political. In July 1949 Werner becomes an SED candidate. In the CV that he hands in with his application to become a Party member, he writes: "My period of study at teacher-training college helped me to find my class position." It is a different Werner writing here, a fresh convert. At home the red flag now flies in the window. Werner also buys two flags for his father-in-law Fritz, with whom he has fallen out again because suddenly Fritz doesn't seem Communist enough to the newly aligned Werner. Werner passes his diploma with merit, and in 1950 he is appointed senior adviser at the main school authority. He organizes the political work in the vocational schools. Young people are to be won over for the newly founded GDR. That is, he is told, more important than any subject teaching. Werner goes from school to school, agitates, explains, persuades and writes assessments and recommendations. Non-political headmasters are replaced by Party members, politically dubious teachers are fired. Everything is turned on its head, and everything has to start over again. Werner works till he drops, he often spends the night in the office so as not to waste any time. It has to be done quickly, the Cold War is in full swing, and Berlin has become its main stage. Werner assembles agitation units who go to West Berlin to persuade the people there of the rightness of the cause. They stand at crossroads handing out flyers. Once, at Bülowplatz, they are beaten up "by an enemy unit". They return to the East with bruises and torn clothes, convinced more than ever of the aggression of imperialism.

At the weekends Werner works as a volunteer in the reconstruction of Berlin, shifts stones, pours foundations, builds window frames and doors. He works over a hundred half-shifts in 1952 alone. I have in front of me his "reconstruction notebook", in which every shift is stamped. In the summer he sometimes moves rubble even after work. "Every hour of reconstruction a patriotic deed," it says in the notebook. By way of recognition Werner is awarded the Reconstruction Badge Grade II. There is a photograph of Werner, taken at the May Day demonstration in 1952. Werner is walking along the street in a light-coloured, tailored suit, with a GDR banner over his shoulder. Werner is taller than all the other demonstrators, and seems to be beaming inwardly. I can imagine them wanting someone like that in their own ranks. He emanates strength and determination.

A short time later Werner is appointed head of the woodcraft school, and six months later the teaching body puts him forward for the title of "Meritorious Teacher of the People". In an official statement the other teachers write: "In taking over our school, the Headmaster found a tendency towards group formation among the teaching body. With great logic and persistence the Headmaster put in place the beginnings of a teachers' collective. The whole of the teaching body took part in the circle he ran for the study of the classics of Marxism–Leninism." That means that Werner isn't just running a school, he is also shaping people, just as he himself has just been shaped. They sit together in their free time and read Marx. His school "is to be an expression of the new society", he reports to the main school authority in June 1952. And he means it.

In January 1953 Werner is given a special honour. He receives a letter from the Central Committee of the SED. The comrades write: "In recognition of your achievement in the construction of our democratic school system, you have been granted a flat in our first Socialist street, the Stalinallee. We wish to congratulate you and hope that you will be happy in your new home." Werner even kept his housing allocation form. Stalinallee Block B South, third floor right. The flat is handed over on Stalin's seventy-third birthday. There is a ceremony in the Staatsoper, to which the first 1,148 tenants are invited. The mayor, Friedrich Ebert, delivers a speech. The newspaper *Neues Deutschland* publishes a list of all the names. "These are the people our Republic needs. Hard-working, dogged, dynamic," writes the central organ of the SED. Werner has become a kind of prototype of the Socialist citizen.

Werner has a folder containing the certificates that he has acquired over the years. His appointment as senior teacher, as *Studienrat*, the award of the Pestalozzi medal for loyal service in bronze and silver,

Werner (second from the left) at the May Day demonstration, 1952

for the title Socialist Labour Activist. What a rise. Werner is showing himself and everyone else that the son of a worker can really achieve something in this new state. After all the years of imprisonment, of humiliation, of being lost, he is suddenly in the front row, he has become an important, respected man. He no longer needs to look back, he now looks straight ahead.

In his private life, too, Werner is making changes. In November 1951 he divorces Sigrid and a year later marries the policeman's daughter Hildegard, with whom he had been in love for some time. They have a daughter called Karola, to whom Werner is lovingly devoted. He is no longer aggressive, the tension has gone, because he's content at last. His old family is slowly forgotten. There is no room for Wolf, his sister Rita and Sigrid in Werner's new life. He gradually forgets all about them. His daughter Karola says Werner was never ill intentioned, he just repressed everything. "He's quite good at that, deliberately repressing things. He decides to do it, and then eventually it's really gone," she says. Karola describes Werner as a trusting man of total honesty, who internalized Socialism and lived it. "You couldn't talk to him about certain problems in the GDR. He just wouldn't have it." Karola isn't allowed to wear jeans, and Western television is strictly forbidden. Werner talks about the new society, about the great future that awaits them all. And in fact, Karola says, he wasn't really a particularly political person. He wanted to achieve something, he wanted to be part of things, and fulfil the tasks he was assigned as well as he possibly could. And he was also grateful to the state that had allowed him to do so much.

Perhaps Werner was a person who would have worked well in more or less any system, in any role. He would always have made the best of things. His life's happiness would not have been threatened if Hitler had won the war, or if he'd happened to end up in the West. He would certainly have been a good stage painter if he hadn't been a good headmaster. Just as he had been a good model-maker, a good soldier, a good prisoner. And now a good citizen of the GDR.

16

Alienations

GERHARD COMES TO EAST BERLIN in January 1952. And not by chance. He is on a secret Party mission that not even his wife is allowed to know about. My mother told me years ago that Gerhard had been involved in Secret Service matters of some kind. She didn't know anything more than that, because even after the end of the GDR Gerhard didn't want to talk about it. Before I started writing this book, I went to Gerhard to ask him if I could see his Stasi file. I wrote the question in the blue notebook on his coffee table. He read it and nodded. I couldn't tell from his expression whether he was pleased or annoyed that I was poking around in his past. He let me get on with it. A few months later this big pack of papers lay on my desk. Two hundred pages of material. I read all night, and the next morning Gerhard had turned into someone else as far as I was concerned. I know you have to be careful with the things in those files, but if only half of what they contain is true, Gerhard was a brave man in the GDR as well. A devout believer, certainly, and loyal to the cause until the bitter end, but also truthful and critical. The very opposite of the ossified functionary that he was in our family. Why did he hide from us for all those years?

*

According to his Stasi file, Gerhard's double life begins in Düsseldorf, where he lives with his family after the war. He works as an editor with the KPD newspaper *Freiheit*, and early in 1950 he receives information about a man who worked for the security service (SD) in the Third Reich, and is now supposed to be working for the Americans. This man arranges to meet him and says he was recruited by the US Army after coming back from a prisoner-of-war camp, to work with other former Gestapo and SD members to set up a new Secret Service in West Germany. Gerhard finds the story shocking and at the same time extremely interesting. He tells his editor-in-chief about it. He says the Party administration should be informed, ideally KPD head Max Reimann in person. Two days later Reimann calls Gerhard in, praises him for this important information and asks him to do further research. Not for an article, however, but for the Party's news agency. From now on his editorial work is just a facade, and Gerhard is an agent. This sounds like a considerable change, but it could be that Gerhard didn't see it that way at all. He was familiar with this sort of thing from his illegal work in France. He just kept going as before. His code name was the same as it had been in France. He calls himself "Paul".

From now on Gerhard regularly meets his informant, who gives him detailed information about the process involved in setting up the West German Secret Service, and gets money in return. Two months later Gerhard becomes a "resident" of the news agency. This means that he is now running a whole network of informants, who have been working for the service for a long time. Almost all of these informants are former SS men who have ended up working in West German politics and administration, and who are being blackmailed by the KPD news agency. They provide secret information for free, and in return the comrades refrain from exposing them. That's the deal.

One of the informants is called August Moritz, a former SS *Obersturmbannführer* who was in France during the war, running the Gestapo divisions in Orléans and Marseilles, amongst other things. In Gerhard's Stasi file he is listed under the name "Kornbrenner". August Moritz is wanted as a war criminal, and living under a false identity in Düsseldorf. In 1954 the military court in Marseilles sentenced him to death because Moritz had had dozens of French civilians and partisans tortured and killed, and helped to organize the deportation of Jews. His mission in Gerhard's network is to locate former SS men and recruit them for the Secret Service.

The first time I read that, I couldn't believe it. Gerhard worked with someone like that? A man who had killed partisans and Jews, and who would have killed Gerhard if he had fallen into his hands in France? How could Gerhard live with himself, protecting a man like that? Nobody can have so much discipline, so much self-control, I thought. Even Markus Wolf, head of the Foreign Policy News Agency APN, which took over the KPD agents in 1951, writes that collaboration with August Moritz was an "almost unconscionable burden" for Gerhard. In the files, however, there is nothing to suggest that "Resident Paul" had any problems with "Kornbrenner". In a report, Gerhard even singles out Moritz's work for praise, and recommends that they go on working with him: "The information is correct, the predicted developments apply. We can draw conclusions from these which will be significant in our struggle for peace and the unity of Germany." Gerhard can clearly keep work and emotions separate. But how much the agent Paul and the human being Gerhard must have made one another suffer.

Paul's network is constantly growing. He now has a secretary and two couriers who bring his reports to East Berlin. In January 1952 Gerhard's informant in the West German Secret Service is transferred to Berlin. The Party decides that Gerhard is to go with him. That is also the reason why the family doesn't come back to Düsseldorf after their winter holiday in Oberhof, and why they are suddenly called Oswald. Gerhard needs the new name because the comrades in Berlin assume the Americans have unmasked him. Three months after Gerhard's transfer, the West German counter-espionage service discover the "Kornbrenner network". August Moritz and four of his former SS comrades are arrested. In December 1953 they are sentenced to several years' imprisonment after the first major trial for treason in the BRD.

Just a few weeks after Gerhard's arrival in East Berlin, the head of espionage, Markus Wolf, starts to examine the networks of the former Party news agency. The whole apparatus is assessed as a "security risk", for which reason Wolf recommends "immediately cleansing the service and phasing it out". According to a report marked "top secret": "Throughout the whole of the old news agency, conspiratorial work, the selection of colleagues and sources, was so careless and badly organized that the enemy must have been fully aware of all of its work, and able to use the apparatus to disorient our own Party leadership. (…) In particular, it is not yet certain to what extent the enemy has been able to use the apparatus to recruit former colleagues, or the extent to which the carelessness that has been uncovered was due to deliberate sabotage. In the case of some former members of staff, this material is very grave and extensive, even though it is less a matter of proof in the judicial sense."

Today some people say that Markus Wolf dissolved the Party's news agency to rid himself of vexatious competition, and at the same time gain valuable sources in the West. All the service staff were subjected to examination. Many of them ended in prison as "traitors" because they knew too much, or because they had become dangerous for some other reason. In a record of a conversation at the Stasi Main Administration Reconnaissance, dated 9 August 1952, it says: "A memorandum about Resident Paul must be prepared by 15.9.1952, so that a decision can be made on whether he is to be withdrawn from service or arrested." Gerhard probably never knew how much danger he was in.

On 18 September 1952 Markus Wolf presents a report on Gerhard. Wolf writes: "Paul's past needs a more thorough examination. If the possibility of deliberate sabotage on his part is left open, it must at any rate be established that he lacks the firm Marxist foundation, that he has never had the opportunity to acquire a real class consciousness, that he is the type of the intellectual with many bourgeois weaknesses and thus, in spite of his intelligence, was not capable of performing the duties of a qualified resident. (…) In France he was in contact with the future renegade Herbert Müller, with the traitor Werner Schwarze and others. Paul's account of his participation in the Resistance movement is romantic and fantastical. (…) In Paul's case it must further be borne in mind that because of his family relationships he has a wide range of acquaintances both at home and abroad, particularly among Trotskyist elements. His Jewish origins cannot go unmentioned here. Paul's work is certainly known to the enemy."

This report could have put Gerhard in jail. Suspicion of sabotage, no real class consciousness, bourgeois weaknesses, contact with traitors, renegades and Trotskyists, and Jewish origin. Other people in those days were thrown out of the Party, arrested or sent to Siberia on the grounds of less serious accusations. The "cleansings" in the Party were in full swing at the time. Commissions were searching for "enemies" and "Western agents". About 150,000 "deviationists" were excluded from the SED in the early Fifties, most of them former Social Democrats. In November 1952 Rudolf Slánský, the former General Secretary of the Czechoslovak Communist Party, was sentenced to death in a show trial. In the GDR, paranoia is clearly mounting as well. Trials are prepared, members of the Politburo and the Central Committee are arrested. Even men like Franz Dahlem, until 1952 the second man in the GDR, or Wilhelm Zaisser, the Minister for State Security, are removed from their posts for "counter-revolutionary activities" and "involvement with imperialist agents". Eugen, Gerhard's closest comrade in the Resistance, whose name is actually Werner Schwarze, is suspected of being a traitor. During those years no one knows for sure, anyone could be an enemy from one day to the next. Suspicion prevails.

This suspicion by the new power-holders even towards their most loyal comrades probably has something to do with their own history. People like Walter Ulbricht and Markus Wolf trusted, if they trusted anyone, only people they knew from their exile in Moscow, who had been through the same things as they had. The others, living as émigrés in the West, who came from bourgeois or Jewish families, who only became Communists during the war, were suspect to them. People like Walter Ulbricht and Markus Wolf had learnt in the Soviet Union how Stalinist terror worked, how a people could be made docile and obedient. You have to imagine how they felt when they came home from Moscow after the war. They never forgot that the people they were now ruling were the very same people who had once driven them from Germany. It was clear to them that these people could be governed only by force and with strict controls. State security, the spy state, a society organized along military lines, were the consequences of deep mistrust towards their own people.

Strangely, not much happens to Gerhard. He is no longer able to work for the Secret Service, but he's now a journalist with the

ADN news agency, running their department for pan-German affairs. And the Stasi have their eye on him. In a report for Stasi Main Administration V, dated 4 December 1954, it says: "At ADN Leo has been saying negative things about measures of the Central Committee of the SED. He is calling for 'press freedom' in the GDR. Leo is a loose cannon. The KP 'Elvira' is given the mission, as she is in contact with Leo through her work, of pinning him down, establishing his contacts, so as to be able to introduce operational measures on our part." At the end of the report is the note: "Leo was an émigré to the West and is a Jew." Another observation about his Jewish origins. It makes me flinch every time.

Gerhard's landlady in Friedrichshagen is questioned by the Stasi, and colleagues are asked to give assessments of his character on various pretexts. In June 1955 the Stasi Major Paul Kienberg observes: "Nothing suspicious has been discovered from the personal milieu. Leo is usually picked up by car very early in the morning, and doesn't come home until late at night. Any free time he devotes to his family. The flat is well furnished, but not super-modern or extravagant. The furnishings are the bourgeois norm. Various colleagues in his ADN department are aware that Leo stays away from social life. The Party group and the central Party administration have spoken to Leo on several occasions, from which it has emerged that he is alienated from the Party. The Party leadership is considering releasing Leo from his job. The appropriate measures are also being contemplated in the Party."

A loose cannon, alienated from the Party. In a report dated February 1956, Major Kienberg demands "the extension of operational measures". At the top left of the first page of the report it says in black ink: "Do not share concerns. Immediately impose measures." The signature is indecipherable. From that day Gerhard is no longer under surveillance, there are no further reports from people who have been put on his case. Who has been protecting him? It must have been someone with great influence, because the management of the ADN no longer want to fire him, and even the Party no longer sees a reason to punish him. Six words in black ink were enough to stop the machinery.

Did Gerhard not feel the noose tightening around him? Did he know about the accusations, about his reprieve? He probably didn't know anything at all. That's the only explanation for why he went on talking quite blithely and openly. For example on 17 September 1956 in the Berlin press café with two colleagues. One of them is a secret member of staff (GM) of the Stasi, and he informs Major Kienberg about the conversation. Kienberg writes in his report: "Leo said we must, as in Hungary, collect signatures to bring about a change in the Party leadership. In answer to the GM's question of who, in his opinion, should be considered as new members, Leo replied evasively that there were quite enough people."

Gerhard clearly wasn't used to suspecting his own people. He'd never had that before. In France the comrades had been people he could always depend upon, to whom he had entrusted his life because the important thing was to defeat the Nazis. In Düsseldorf the enemy was the Americans. Now, in Berlin, the battles were different. This time it wasn't partisans, but functionaries. It was comrades versus other comrades. There were impenetrable power struggles, intrigues, propaganda campaigns. It's actually impossible that Gerhard knew nothing about any of this, that he was unaware of the fear that prevailed everywhere.

And Gerhard? In August 1956 he went to Hungary on official business, and met people from the Petőfi Circle in the evening. This was a discussion group of young Hungarian literati substantially involved in the preparation of the popular uprising that would break out only two months later. The Stasi learnt of Gerhard's contact with the enemy. Several informal colleagues reported on the evening in Budapest. A report dated 6.12.1956 says: "During a stay in Hungary he made contact with the Petőfi Circle and also took part in political discussions in the Petőfi Club. Leo introduced himself there and welcomed the political debates. He thanked a speaker who was highly critical of Hungary's politics for this discussion, and thought it was correct." A memo signed by one Lieutenant Reuter reports on a Party assembly at the ADN which took place a few weeks later. "Leo openly put forward the opinion that the counter-revolutionary events in Poland in 1956 had been provoked not by the enemy, but by discussions within the Polish Workers' Party. He is thus clearly and deliberately defying the Party line, which does not seem to matter to him in the slightest."

Was Gerhard being particularly brave or particularly gullible, or both? Did he know that someone was protecting him, and did he therefore take more liberties than most other people? Or was that normal for him? Did the Stasi deliberately create a bogeyman who didn't really exist? Did they turn him into a renegade so that they could punish him more easily later? I don't know, and will probably never find out. But when I read these reports and assessments I feel proud of my grandfather. I've always wondered why he was so brave in France and later, in the East, didn't open his mouth. Now I know that at least he wasn't one of the ones who simply went along with everything. That he defended himself when the lies and the stupidity became too obvious. But why weren't his family allowed to know anything about this, why did he always act the model comrade? Why did he not allow his children to have the doubts that he had himself? Perhaps he was afraid of showing weakness. After all, he had been taught always to maintain his composure, and to express criticism, if at all, only within the Party, so as not to play into the hands of the enemy. Eventually he probably confided more to the Party than he did to his children.

And he probably wasn't quite as gullible after he'd understood how the big idea worked in the little GDR. The Stasi files contain the record of a Party discussion held with Gerhard. The paper isn't dated, but since it is about events in Poland and Hungary, I assume it must come from 1956. The comrades accuse Gerhard of not toeing the Party line sufficiently, of putting forward his own opinion when he should really be representing the views of the Party. According to this report Gerhard says: "I agree that in critical situations only one thing matters in work: discipline. That in work you sometimes have to implement things that you're not currently convinced about, or, as Comrade Müller once said in a situation that was critical for me, that one must obey. But we have the Party, to which you can tell your concerns and whatever's making you unhappy." Did they give him a nudge, or did he really think that? Obeying, doing things you don't believe in. Was that what he had fought for? How did he cope with it, with that constraint, with that suspicion? Why did almost all of them play along with that horrible game, the brave fighters who came back to the GDR after the war?

I once had a conversation with Gerhard about it. That is, it wasn't really a conversation, it was an interview that we both gave to a French magazine years after the fall of the Wall. It was about grandfathers and grandsons in the GDR. In that interview Gerhard spoke for the first time about guilt, and he explained why people like himself were so attached to the country. He talked about the hope he had after the war. About the hope of building a new society in which the Nazis would never again have a chance. He had seen, he said, that there were war criminals in the government in West Germany, and that mass murderers were drawing high pensions. That could never have happened in the GDR. It would have been more important than anything else. His hope had allowed him to put up with some things that were actually unbearable. That was the price of the new, those had been the necessary sacrifices, and in the end the cause was always more important than the individual, he always used to say.

It must have been like a litany, a constant attempt at self-persuasion. And would his whole struggle not have been in vain if he had suddenly stopped being involved? Because that GDR was the result of the struggle, the reward. The point of life. He couldn't get out of it without losing himself. "That was my country," he said in that interview. And it sounded sad, but also a bit proud. And I reflected that it couldn't be my country for precisely that reason. But I said nothing. And everything was exactly as it had been before.

I think that for both my grandfathers the GDR was a kind of dreamland, in which they could forget all the depressing things that had gone before. It was a new start, a chance to begin all over again. The persecution, the war, the imprisonment, all the terrible things that Gerhard and Werner had been through could be buried under that huge pile of the past. From now on all that mattered was the future. And trauma turned to dream. The idea of building an anti-fascist state had a beneficial effect on both of them. Gerhard could devote himself to the illusion that GDR citizens were very different Germans from the ones that had once driven his family out of the country. And Werner could act as if he had always believed in Socialism. All wounds, all mistakes were forgotten and forgiven if you were willing to become part of this new society.

New faith for old suffering: that was the ideal behind the foundation of the GDR.

That is the explanation for the unbounded loyalty with which Gerhard and Werner were bound to that country until the bitter end. They could never unmask the great dream as a great lie because the lies they needed to live would have been exposed at the same time.

And their children? They were hurled into their fathers' dreamlands, and had to dream along whether they wanted to or not. They didn't know that founding ideal. And because they had nothing to overcome, nothing to hide, they found faith difficult too. They saw the poverty, the lies, the claustrophobia, the suspicion. And they heard their fathers' phrases as they raved about the future. Much of the power and the euphoria had gone. And the grandchildren? They were glad when it was all over. They didn't even have a guilty conscience at kicking the state. What did I get from the great dream? Small-minded prohibitions, petty principles and jeans that looked like elongated Youth Front shirts. The energy of the state had been used up in three generations. The GDR remained the country of old men, of the founding fathers, and their logic no longer made sense to anybody.

17

Collisions

WHEN I WAS SIX, I had my first brush with the Stasi. A crash, in fact. I was on my way back from playing with a friend, I ran across the road and was hit by a car. Wolf later told me that the impact had knocked off the car's number plate, revealing a second one underneath. It was all very unpleasant for the driver. Not only had he hit a child, he also had to explain to the traffic policeman and the witnesses why there were cars with two number plates in the GDR. Wolf said that jerk of a Stasi had been driving far too fast. At the time I didn't know what Stasi meant, but I can say that my relationship with them wasn't a good one from the outset.

I was taken to the A & E hospital in Prenzlauer Berg and had to have an operation on my spleen. I spent six weeks in a room on the ground floor, with barred windows, although that had nothing to do with the Stasi. My parents were only allowed to visit me once a week. To keep me from getting too excited, the doctors said. Wolf came more often, he climbed up the bars and waved at me from outside. I can't remember if I thought that was nice or sad. Or whether it was exciting. But I've kept that image of my father behind the barred window. It's one of my very earliest memories. When I told Westerners about the GDR after the fall of the Wall, the barred

Maxim on his first day at school, 1976

window always came up. The Westerners loved that story, because it was exactly the way they imagined the GDR. A child being hit by a Stasi car and separated from its parents, alone in a barred room.

Childhood pictures came to me whose meanings I only understood later on. There was the road in Wandlitz on which cars weren't allowed, which was why we could have slalom bicycle races with our hands off the handlebars. The street led through a beech wood to Lake Liepnitz. In the forest there was a green painted wall, hung with signs saying "Wild Animal Research Area". Wolf said that big, dangerous animals lived behind the wall. I thought of lions and dragons, and was always slightly scared when we cycled to Lake Liepnitz. I wasn't sure if the wall was high enough to keep the monsters away from us. Eventually Wolf explained that the big animals were the people who governed the country, and the wall in the forest was only there to protect them from us. I asked who could be afraid of us, and Wolf said the men who lived in the forest were afraid of everything. On Lake Liepnitz there was a peninsula where no one was allowed to go because, it was said, only Erich Honecker was allowed to swim there. Our swimming spot wasn't far from that peninsula. I'd have liked to see what Erich Honecker looked like in swimming trunks. But he was never there. The big jetty lay deserted in the sun. Anne said Erich Honecker probably had no time to go swimming, because he always had to make sure that everything in our country was going according to plan. I felt sorry for Erich Honecker, because it was really a lovely spot to go swimming. Once two boys swam over, trying to get to the jetty. But before they reached the shore, soldiers with sub-machine guns were standing there, shouting at them to turn around straight away because the peninsula was a restricted area.

I thought restricted areas were exciting. There was one on the Baltic as well. In the May holidays we often went to Prerow, where there was a camping site in the dunes. The nudist block which Anne and Wolf always wanted to go to was bounded by a barbed-wire fence. Beyond it the border area began. Once, when the weather was bad, two friends and I dug a deep hole in the sand of the dunes not far from the barbed-wire fence. By the end the hole was deeper than we were tall. We needed a rope ladder to get back out. The next day there was great agitation. Soldiers with Alsatians stood by the hole, demanding to know who had dug it. My friends and I said nothing, and the soldiers filled the hole with their shovels. Wolf was agitated too. He told us not to dig our holes by the fence in future, because the soldiers might think we were trying to escape to the West.

Escape to the West. That was one of my favourite games. It took at least four of you. Three children lined up by the climbing frame; they were the border guards. The fourth had to try to get past the border guards and climb the frame. Once you'd made it to the other side, you had to shout "West", and you'd won. Once we went to the Brandenburg Gate with our class. I was eight years old. The teacher wanted to show us the "Anti-Fascist Protection Rampart". While our teacher was talking about the Socialist fight for freedom, we wondered about the easiest way of getting over there. With a crane, somebody suggested, or with a glider, said somebody else. The next day we write a local geography essay on the subject of "Why the State Border Must Be Protected". Anne has kept my local geography exercise file from the third class of primary school. I have in front of me the lined page with the pre-printed question. I wrote: "Because otherwise everybody would run away and because there are fascists over there." I only got a Three for it. The correct answer is written next to it in red ink: "So that freedom is secured."

Flicking through that file today, the memory comes flooding back. The leather smell of my schoolbag, the hairdo of my class teacher Frau Pankratz, the loudspeaker voice of Headmaster Griebsch at the flag ceremony, my first Pioneer card and the face of Peggy Sadzinsky, who sat two desks in front of me. I find dried leaves, a piece of paper listing the most important features of the domestic pig, photographs of Sigmund Jähn and Valery Bykovsky, who had just come back from space, and my Pioneer mission, in which I undertook to participate in the Week of Socialist Solidarity, and to stop spitting in Ninette Reinel's face. One page is headed: "What we have achieved since the foundation of the GDR". It is a list in table form: "Everything belongs to the state, and the state is us. Everyone has the right to participate. Life is good and very good. No job worries. The capitalists and warmongers are disempowered. More and more new apartments, Saturdays off."

There are other tables in the file, showing how bad things were for workers in the past, and how marvellous they are now, how terrible the living conditions of people in Russia were before the October Revolution, and how much of a paradise it became afterwards. I learnt it all off by heart and then wrote essays in class and then I forgot it again. Just as I have forgotten the most important characteristics of the domestic pig and the leaves of the ten most familiar deciduous trees. In later school years there were many more tables. The three determining factors of a revolutionary situation, ten reasons for the superiority of Socialism, the five most important points of the first SED Party programme. Listless teachers wrote the tables on the board, listless pupils wrote them in their notebooks, listless parents signed off the classwork. That was Socialism as it reached me. Phrases in table form.

At break we swapped *Bravo* posters and Duplo stickers and talked about the most recent episodes of *Gunsmoke*. I don't think any of us gave a thought to how it all fitted together. The American television series, the West German *Bravo* posters and the superiority of Socialism. It was somehow clear that there was one truth at school and another in real life. You just had to switch over. Like on television.

Later we moved to Karlshorst, where it was quieter and greener than in Prenzlauer Berg. We lived in a two-family house and had a small garden. Upstairs was old Frau Kaiser, whose house it was. We only had to cross one street to get to school, which had been important to Anne and Wolf since my accident. In the new school there was a flag ceremony once a month. Just before it began, we put on our FDJ shirts, and as the last sounds of the GDR national anthem faded away we took them off again. I don't think it was a protest, it was just that it was extremely uncool to wear an FDJ shirt.

I remember how surprised my grandfather Gerhard once was when I told him how it was at our school. The subject arose because he had seen the West German plastic bag in which I hid my FDJ shirt in my schoolbag. Gerhard told me about his time in the Red Falcons. They had worn blue shirts at the time too, and he liked going to the gatherings with the others and suddenly being in the middle of a blue sea. I liked this image of a blue sea, but I knew gatherings like that would scare me.

One day in November 1982 our headmistress Frau Reichenbach hurried into our changing room. We had just finished games. Frau Reichenbach had tears in her eyes and said, "Something terrible has happened. The Soviet General Secretary Leonid Brezhnev is dead." For a moment there was silence, and then we couldn't help giggling, because Kai Petzold was standing naked behind Frau Reichenbach, desperately looking for his underpants. Frau Reichenbach didn't understand what was going on, she could just hear us giggling and furiously left the room. In the class after that we were supposed to have maths, but Frau Reichenbach came into our class and said that after what had happened each of us had to write an essay about Leonid Brezhnev. It turned out that few of us knew who he was. And then Frau Reichenbach started crying again, and she shouted that there would be consequences. But nothing at all happened, except that another Soviet leader died a few months later and nobody at school told us.

A few people from our class went to Scripture classes every week. One of them was a girl I was slightly in love with, so I decided to go too. In the church there was a room fitted with thick carpets. In the middle of the room there were five big candles, and we sat in a circle on the floor and listened to the vicar, Irene, telling us stories about Jesus. They were nice stories, and everyone listened intently, not at all like in school. There were prayers at the end of the class, which was always a little unpleasant because I didn't actually believe in God. But there was something attractive and mysterious about it. I told my mother, who was startled because she didn't know why I was suddenly interested in religion. I noticed that Anne had a problem with it, which gave my interest in Scripture classes a real boost. Once I even prayed in bed at night. I can't remember what I said, but I was quite excited because I didn't know if there was someone somewhere listening to me.

In Scripture classes Irene explained that you had to love your neighbour as yourself. Beside me was a fat girl from the other class who always sweated terribly, and with the best will in the world I couldn't imagine how I was supposed to love that girl. Other Christian principles that Irene talked to us about struck me as strange. That you're not supposed to fight back if somebody starts hitting you, for example. That made about as much sense as the Socialism tables at school. Scripture classes were on Tuesday. And Wednesday was FDJ afternoon. In year seven Frau Reichenbach decided to move the FDJ afternoon to Tuesdays, because she thought the children at her school should make their minds up. Church or FDJ. The result was that the following Tuesday half of our class went to Scripture lessons, whereupon the old timetable was immediately reinstated. Then Irene said that faith had won, but I thought we'd actually won.

From year seven onwards we had a class called "Productive Work" once a week. We went to a metal plant that made parts for gas boilers. The people there probably didn't know what to do with us, so we had to spend hours sorting screws which, once we had gone, were all jumbled again to keep the next class busy. After a while, instead of going to the plant, a few of my mates and I sometimes went to the wood that started just behind our park. On the edge of the wood there was a Soviet barracks. The soldiers who patrolled in front of the barracks walls gave us cigarettes with a cardboard filter so strong that I couldn't even smoke them without inhaling. The soldiers were always pleased to see us. They said, "Home far, children far, women far," and we understood that they felt rather lonely here. Lots of Russians lived in Karlshorst. You could spot them immediately when they came towards you on the pavement. The women wore lots of make-up and wore thick fur hats on their heads even in spring. The men wore sand-brown uniforms, which were usually too big. The soldiers in the wood were sometimes drunk. They offered us some of their vodka, but we didn't dare try it. The people in Karlshorst said the Russians drank alcohol that made you blind. Once on New Year's Eve drunk Russian soldiers threw grenades into a campfire. One of them was said to have lost both legs and both arms. The others were beaten by their superiors and ended up in jail. People said the Russian soldiers were poor bastards, and yet they were probably happy to be in Karlshorst because things were even worse in Russia. I didn't understand that because the Russians had won the war. There were films on television showing the heroic struggle of the Red Army. I knew that Hitler would never have been defeated without the

Red Army. That they'd liberated us. But the soldiers in Karlshorst didn't look like victors.

When I was fifteen the boys from our year were supposed to go to a pre-military training camp. The girls were allowed to stay at home and train as paramedics. My mother thought it was terrible that we were supposed to be drilled for the army at such a young age. She got hold of a medical certificate declaring me physically unfit. But I didn't like the idea of staying at home with the girls. I wanted to go to the camp and kept on at Anne until she let me go. We went to a garrison village near Berlin. On the first day we had to lock our clothes in a cupboard, we were given green uniforms and told that over the next two weeks they would make men of us, which didn't strike me as bad at all. But at the time I didn't know that men get up at six in the morning and run three kilometres before they have breakfast. The rest of the day we crawled through the wood, learnt to march in time and to protect ourselves against a nuclear flash. It was all very easy: you just had to throw yourself on the ground and cover yourself with a tarpaulin, and nothing could happen.

Our woodwork teacher Herr Krück, who took us to the military camp, turned out to be a man who values discipline and order over everything else. Every evening we had to polish our black military boots until they gleamed, fold our uniforms neatly and stand by our beds. In normal life Herr Krück was a small, quiet man who sat in his workshop in his blue overalls and was happy to be left alone. Now he strutted about like a general and barked orders. I thought about the easy time I could have had with the girls in Berlin, and swore always to listen to my mother from now on. Twice a week politkommissars from the People's Army came and told us about the military situation. The officers demonstrated possible front lines and war scenarios. The starting point for these reflections was always a night-time ambush by imperialist Nato troops. I hadn't been aware until then that we had so many enemies, all just waiting to destroy us in a moment of weakness. The only reason, the officers explained, why the enemy hadn't risked an attack before, was the strength of our troops. But that strength couldn't be taken for granted, at that difficult time more than any other the Republic needed young people who were prepared to defend their country. Lists were distributed, on which we could apply to volunteer for a longer period of military service. I don't know whether it was the fact that I'd just spent two weeks crawling around the area in uniform, or because the polit-kommissars talked to us in such a friendly, serious way, but I actually considered signing up. Then it occurred to me that three years in the army might also mean being sent to the border, and I wanted to avoid that under any circumstances.

On the second-last day in the army camp we were allowed to fire a sub-machine gun. Each of us got five cartridges, the gun had to be set to single fire, and we had to shoot at a picture of a soldier about fifty metres away. I was so excited that all my shots missed, but I was still proud. When I got home I told Wolf about shooting practice. He got incredibly agitated because he hadn't known that we were doing such dangerous things in the camp. I said it had been great and he should calm down, but the next day Wolf ran to my headmistress Frau Reichenbach and yelled that this bloody school was forcing children to use guns. That got Anne worked up in turn, because the selection procedure for Abitur delegation was going on at the time. "You've just fucked up your son's future," she said. And Wolf told her it was this bloody state that was fucking up people's futures.

It was through my parents that I found out how things really worked. It was just a bit confusing because the two of them rarely agreed about anything. Wolf said the GDR was a dictatorship of civil servants who had betrayed Socialism. Anne said there were definitely big problems, but they could be overcome. As a rule political discussions with me turned into an argument between the two of them, in the course of which Wolf's position became considerably more radical. He started talking about the "criminal state" and the "GDR prison", and Anne said in a tone of warning that he only made things harder if he said things like that. So I had a pretty good idea what I had to say and where if I wanted to avoid getting into trouble. I always got top marks in citizenship because we had all those tables. I went to FDJ propaganda meetings and at home I read copies of *Der Spiegel* that my mother sometimes secretly brought home from work. I was proud to have been initiated into my parents' secrets without my teachers noticing. My mother particularly liked to tell me about historical connections, because she herself thought they were the most important thing. She said she wanted me to have it easier than she had, and if possible know the truth before other people told lies. I knew for example that on 17 June 1953 there had been a workers' uprising in East Berlin, which had been brutally suppressed by the Soviet Army. And in class I wrote that it had been counter-revolutionary provocateurs and West German agents who had wanted to damage the working class of the GDR. And I didn't even have to fight with myself to do it, I didn't feel like a traitor or a coward for saying what other people wanted to hear from me.

Perhaps it was because none of it was really very important to me. Not important enough to take a risk or put myself at a disadvantage for. Today I know how much pain every genuflection, every compromise, must have caused Anne, because she felt connected to the GDR, because she wanted to change things. For her, every lie was a defeat, because she wanted to be honest with the state. Even my father says he'd always hoped that something would happen in this country, because the situation had never really been hopeless. I didn't feel that way. I had more of a non-relationship with the state. After everything my parents had told me about the GDR, after everything I'd seen of it myself, I had stopped caring about it. I don't think I was ever really aware of that. But thinking about it today, it strikes me that I didn't actually have any real feelings about the country. There was neither hatred nor love, neither hope nor disappointment. Just a kind of numb indifference.

That might sound strange, because everybody feels something about his home. But I had separated my feelings of home from the GDR: the birch tree outside our summer house in Basdorf, the swimming spot on Lake Liepnitz, the lake park in Karlshorst, the street where I was born, had nothing to do with this state as far as I was concerned. The GDR was other people. My headmistress Frau Reichenbach, the civil servants who stood on the stage at the May Day demonstration, the policemen with the Saxon dialect and the presenter of *Aktuelle Kamera*. The GDR was the prohibitions, the idiotic rules, the red banners in the street saying "My hand for my product" or "As we work today, so shall we live tomorrow". My parents taught me to have as little contact as possible with that GDR, to keep my distance. We didn't need to talk about it, it was clear enough already. I saw how Anne and Wolf lived, how they kept the state off their backs. It's only now that I've really understood how attached Anne was to the GDR. She says she didn't want to pass that feeling on to me because it had caused her so much suffering.

Anne talked to me seriously and often, as if talking to an adult. She never tried to convince me, she wanted me to be able to know, to understand, to classify. Once I told her about my feeling in the army camp, when I was on the point of signing myself up for a

Maxim and Wolf, Lake Liepnitz, 1971

longer period of military service. It was a very strange feeling, a need to belong. Today I would say it was an urge to arrive in the GDR. Anne said at the time that there were various ways of living in this country. You could join in or you could resist. You could also join in a bit and resist a bit. Anne said she would always support me, whichever option I went for. But I should clearly understand that you had to be very strong to defend yourself seriously. And that it's hard to stop once you've seriously joined in. Then she looked at me sadly. Perhaps she was thinking about how absurd it is to have to explain things like that to your children.

All of these are moments which, telling them now, assume a meaning that I don't think they had for me at the time. The truth is that my life was mostly normal. As normal as it might have been in Hamburg, or Bonn. So normal that you could simply forget the

GDR. That life was played out at home, in the garden, by the sea, at friends' houses, at the football pitch. It was about jumping from a climbing frame, catching a fish, smoking your first cigarette and snogging girls in the park. It was only later, when I found it harder to avoid the GDR, when it got too close to me, that I started seeing it with different eyes.

18

Trivia

I N WINTER 1976 Anne and Wolf start getting visits from a
young man who introduces himself as a member of staff from
the Education Department of the National People's Army. The
man is called Rainer, and Wolf says he immediately struck him as
sympathetic. Rainer says they had made some enquiries and knew
that Wolf was a critical but committed citizen. So he has a question. Rainer talks about his work, about the scouts in the West who
provided his office with information about the military situation in
the Federal Republic. He said that information was important to
protect the GDR from attack. To preserve peace. The comrades,
who were taking great risks with their work, need support, Rainer
says. It's a trivial matter, but lots of trivia can produce something
big in the end. To cut a long story short, would Anne and Wolf be
willing to make their letter box available in case the comrades in the
West had an important piece of information to pass on. Anne asks
how that would work, and Rainer explains that they wouldn't have
to do anything but call him up if a postcard from a stranger in the
West turned up in their letter box. Then he would come and collect
the card himself.

*

At that moment something happens that Anne and Wolf haven't really been able to explain, even today: they don't refuse, they hesitate, they're willing to think about it, to meet up with Rainer again. When Wolf walks Rainer to the door he says it's actually the least they can do. They bid each other a cordial farewell, as if they were friends from now on.

On his next visit Rainer brings a colleague along. He asks if he could make a call to the West from their house. Just a very quick one. Anne and Wolf feel as if they've been ambushed, but don't dare refuse the request. Rainer's colleague registers a long-distance call, but it doesn't happen. After that they don't hear from Rainer for a while, and no postcards arrive. A few weeks later Rainer calls again and asks if he could have the key to their flat so that his colleagues could use the telephone when they're not at home. Today Wolf says that by this point the whole thing had started feeling far too weird. When Rainer asks about the key again, Anne explains that they don't want to do that, because it's not what they originally discussed. To her astonishment there are no problems or reproaches. Rainer comes once more. They have to sign a piece of paper, undertaking not to say a word about these contacts. Then it's over.

What happened to my parents in the winter of 1976? What made them do things that they didn't actually want to do? They're both embarrassed about the story because it's so inexplicable, because it doesn't fit with the image they have of themselves. Wolf most of all, the rebel, who was never afraid of doing what he thought was right, is still surprised at himself. "They caught me on a side that made it hard to say no," he explains. "That man was nice and discreet, and I didn't feel as if I was dealing with the enemy. And I thought that if you're not going to escape to the West, you have to do something where you are." Anne says she was above all relieved that they didn't want anything more from them. If they had wanted her to spy on people, she'd have turned the idea down flat. But she thought helping scouts in the West was actually OK. "Perhaps we were worried about looking like enemies if we didn't go along with it," she says.

I can't remember exactly when my parents first told me this story. It must have been after the Wall came down. We were talking about Stasi investigations, and Anne thought you ought to go on the offensive where your own story was concerned, and you couldn't keep anything quiet. In Anne's Stasi file there's a personality profile of Wolf produced by the Reconnaissance Department of the Ministry of National Defence before the first contact had been made: "His fundamental attitude towards the GDR is positive. He actively participated in the social work in his residential area, and thus made a considerable contribution to the establishment of the house community. At particularly important socio-political events he made himself voluntarily available. L. is not yet a member of a party. He has a harmonious marriage with his wife and lives with her in orderly family circumstances. He has two children with her. L. was brought to the Reconnaissance Department's attention by an official notification."

Plainly they had seen something in Wolf that he himself did not want to see. The side they'd caught him on, in fact, which you just had to scratch a bit to bring something to light. He had that need to do something, to commit himself, not always just to be against, but also to be for something. If the comrades had been a bit cleverer, if they hadn't startled him with their demands, Wolf might have been willing to do more than even he himself could have imagined.

These stories about the letter box and the telephone were probably just a test to see how far Anne and Wolf would go. My parents'

Wolf, 1976

files are later passed on to Stasi Main Department II, the one responsible for counter-espionage. The Stasi find Wolf interesting too. "His attitude is critical, but not hostile," reads one memo. Another attempt at recruitment begins. "Based on the experience of the Reconnaissance Administration of the Ministry of National Defence, unofficial contact should be made with the couple under false pretences. In the attempt to make an appointment it became apparent that the couple are not prepared to talk to the Security Ministry while preserving the conspiracy. They insisted on meeting on official Security Ministry premises. Wolf Leo spoke openly about his contact with the Reconnaissance Administration, describing it as an 'unconscionable burden'. Under these circumstances no further attempts at contact were made."

I'm trying to imagine what would have happened if Wolf hadn't dared to rebuff the Stasi. It would have gone on like that, step after step, little by little. Lots of people did that, and most of them felt they hadn't really done anything bad. Just a few notes, a little bit of information that probably wasn't important anyway. That didn't hurt anybody, as they always say. You didn't necessarily have to jump through hoops to work for the Stasi. They were keen on people who were different. The little rebels who wanted to change something but didn't know how to go about it. The little know-alls nobody listened to. Wolf could easily have fallen for it. He would have become a Stasi man and still stayed himself. Everything would have made sense at first, and later on he wouldn't have been able to make head or tail of it.

The Stasi files also refer to an "illegal round table (association)" in which Anne and Wolf had taken part in October and November 1977. This round table met once a month at the flat of an acquaintance of my parents in Treptow, and Anne says today that she had no idea at the time that things like that were illegal. Anne and Wolf went there twice. "Problems in journalism were discussed, with content directed against the policy of our Party and government. Wolf Leo was extremely negative in this regard, warning of the infiltration of the Security Ministry in groups of this kind," it says in the report. So Wolf does know that it isn't entirely safe to take part in such round-table discussions. And he's right. As my parents would learn, of the ten participants in the discussions, four are working as Stasi informants. And there's a bug in the chandelier in the sitting room where they meet. Such trouble! And, Anne says, everything was completely harmless, otherwise she wouldn't have gone. Wolf just thought it was boring. A short time later the circle broke up, because the host was getting scared. There was a farewell party at which an incredible number of photographs were taken. A few weeks later the Stasi visit Anne. They want to show her a few pictures to clear up the identity of certain individuals "so that they don't fall through our fingers". Plainly the Stasi still believe that my parents are on their side.

Anne doesn't look at the Stasi pictures. Two weeks later the host of the round table loses his job at the Academy of Sciences and is demoted to the city archive, to which a lot of other people have also been transferred for disciplinary reasons. Nothing happens to Anne and Wolf. They are amazed by all this, because their round table really was completely harmless. A friend tells them it's not about what's discussed in such a group. Forming a group is illegal already. Ten people in a flat are a crime against the state.

At this point Anne is working in the editorial office of the foreign-policy magazine *Horizont*. That was where she really wanted to end up after her studies. Here, she thinks, she can finally realize her dream of competent, incorruptible journalism. But she soon realizes that there are hardly any journalists working in the office. Most of them come from the Party and government apparatus, including many former Secret Service people. The various departments in the magazine are directly answerable to the relevant specialist departments in the Central Committee and the Foreign Ministry. That's where they decide what's going to be published and how it must be written. Compared to what Anne encounters here, the *Berliner Zeitung* was the voice of libertarianism.

Once she writes an article about the crimes of Pol Pot in Cambodia. The article is held back by the Central Committee, because Cambodia is still officially counted among the brother states. Anne complains and asks if the GDR really wants to fraternize with dictators who massacre their own people. There is sympathy within the Central Committee, but the piece is still put on hold for weeks. Until eventually a call comes through. The article is to appear immediately, as a matter of urgency. Anne is delighted, and thinks that honest journalism, exposing crimes, is about to assert itself. Until she works out that that isn't what's happening at all. A week previously, the Chinese had launched an attack on Vietnam, and Cambodia is one of China's supporters. And because solidarity with Vietnam is more important than solidarity with Cambodia, the article can now appear. Once again Anne feels she's being used as part of a political campaign. She thinks about what Wolf is always saying. That everything in this country is nothing but lies and propaganda. And she starts to think about abandoning journalism completely.

The final blow comes at a meeting in which the Party heads of the editorial board are to be re-elected. As always, it's been decided in advance. When the chair of the meeting asks if anyone wants to suggest a candidate, the ones who speak up are the ones who have been told to. All of a sudden Anne has the idea of suggesting a colleague that she values very highly. Everyone's flabbergasted, because nothing like that has ever happened before. The chairman doesn't know if he's even allowed to accept the proposal, so a vote is held. Thirteen colleagues spontaneously decide to support Anne's suggestion. But most are opposed, and everything goes exactly as planned. As far as Anne is concerned, that's that. But a month later, at the next Party meeting, a man from the Central Committee is there, and all the people who voted for Anne's suggestion have to stand up one by one and castigate themselves for their lack of Party discipline. They accuse themselves, demanding punishment for their own unworthy behaviour. Worst of all is the performance of the colleague that Anne suggested as a candidate. He subjects himself to the most severe self-criticism, begs for forgiveness, promises never again to try to be cleverer than the Party. At the end of the meeting fourteen broken men leave the room with their eyes lowered and their shirts drenched in sweat.

Only later Anne finds out that immediately after the Party leadership election an investigating commission in the Central Committee questioned all the dissenters for hours on end. They're talking about a coup, an attack on the Party. But why was she not questioned? Why was she alone spared? A colleague familiar with such matters later explains to her that this tactic is a well-known way of isolating provocateurs. If everybody is punished but the provocateur himself, the others will never want to have anything to do with the person who made life so difficult for them. And from that day onwards none of the people punished ever speak to her again. It's as if she's ceased to exist.

19

Heckling

WOLF EXPERIENCES ALL OF THIS from a distance. When Anne talks about her problems in the kitchen in the evening, he sits there with a questioning expression and can't understand how she puts up with it all. These lies, this anxiety, this strange world that he only knows from her stories. He doesn't understand why she keeps working for that newspaper, in that factory of madness. He tries to shake her awake, to encourage her to risk doing something else. But it doesn't work, he can't get through to her. It's as if there were a wall between them, a border that they can't cross. Today Anne says that that pressure from Wolf made everything even harder. She defended things to him that she had long since stopped believing herself. It was about the principle. She didn't want to swap her father's opinion for her husband's. She wanted to make her own decisions about what she had to do. Wolf says, "The GDR was always there in bed with us."

In our house in Karlshorst, Wolf has set up a studio for himself in the attic. He sits there at his desk, drawing bedtime stories for children which will be shown on GDR television. They're about funny frogs, blonde princesses and bears that stand on their heads. He illustrates books of Russian fairy tales, makes posters for Karl

May western films and colourful postcards covered with nutcrackers and Santa Clauses.

I often went up to see him after school. Nothing ever changed in Wolf's studio. It smelt of glue, paint and coffee. In winter Wolf wore a lambskin waistcoat, in the summer a blue-and-white-striped removal man's shirt that he bought in a professional clothing shop. Sometimes I did my homework up there. It calmed me down to be with him, to hear the scratch of the steel nib on the watercolour card, and the music coming faintly out of the radio. I think he was contended in those days. Whatever was happening outside, here, in the attic, everything was just as he wanted it to be.

In the early Eighties Wolf starts his own artistic projects. It gets started with postcards that he prints himself and sends to friends. The cards are commentaries on the world around him. They are heckles, signs of life in grey and black. A card from 1983 shows a tower of building blocks. A noose is wrapped around one of the legs of the tower. The tower clock stands at just before twelve. On another card a man is crashing his head against a wall until his skull breaks. "Something to think about," is the caption. His New Year card for 1985 shows a GDR sleeping car. "Have a good trip," Wolf writes. On the facade of a new-build block of flats a window is circled. "House arrest" is the title.

It's a long way from funny nutcrackers to cracked skulls. From the colourful cards to the grey ones. They've all been made at around the same time. They belong together.

Wolf has his first exhibition in a bookshop in Karlshorst. In the middle of the room a figure hangs, turning on its own axis. On one wall there are silhouettes of travellers approaching a door that has no handle on the inside. The cross of a window frame casts a shadow, and black crows flap in the darkness. Behind a grating stands a Stasi

Wolf's first exhibition in Karlshorst, 1986

man with a pointed hat. "Leo has a very gloomy view of the present," it says in the Stasi report on the exhibition. In a gallery in Pankow Wolf stages a "non-conversation" between two cardboard figures. A young man slouches casually in a chair, legs crossed, opposite him his pinched father with his legs drawn up. The old man with the hat and the rectangular glasses could be his own father, or he could equally be Gerhard.

But eventually these hidden signs aren't enough for Wolf. He wants to do something, change something. In May 1986 there are elections for the section directors in the Artists' Association. There is a big meeting in the House of Soviet Culture on Friedrichstrasse. On that day Wolf agrees with a few other commercial designers to put up a list of candidates of their own. Just as the steering committee is about to announce the official election proposal, he gets on stage, heart thumping, and makes his own counter-proposal. Wolf tells the assembled colleagues that it's time for them to take control of democracy themselves. He talks about change, of the necessity to start something new with new people. Everyone is so surprised that the suggestion is passed unanimously. And Wolf is as surprised as everybody else that it's all so easy. "You just had to blow, and over everything went, that was a nice experience," he says.

But it isn't without its dangers. Anyone who wants to vote also has to join in with this world of civil servants, and soon the question arises of who's actually changing whom. Wolf is commissioned to design the stage sets for Berlin's 750th anniversary celebrations. This anniversary isn't just any old event. It's one of the highlights in the battle between the systems, because there's a party in West Berlin as well. It's important for the GDR government to present its part of Berlin as a worthy capital of the East German state. And Wolf has become a kind of designer-in-chief of the East Berlin shop window. He says he hasn't really thought much about it. And nobody had talked him into it either. He could do what he liked. He's kept his designs from those days. The stage sets look wild and modern. Red, white and black shapes intersect, flash like thunderbolts over the canvases or link to form long waves. This powerful performance is the opposite of the gloomy world of the GDR that Wolf showed in his exhibitions. Somewhere in between is the country where he lives.

And Wolf hasn't got an entirely free hand either. A poster that he designs for the Party is not printed. The poster shows a pair of sunglasses in which two halves of the city of Berlin are reflected. That's taking things too far for the comrades. Two weeks after the celebrations Wolf is to be awarded the Berlin Prize by the mayor for his work. But Wolf doesn't go to the ceremony. He senses that he's crossed a line, that he's got too close to the powerful men. It's a delicate business, walking the tightrope between acceptance and refusal. "The principle of seduction was always there," says Wolf. "The question constantly arose of how far you can go, how much conformity you can bear without it hurting."

20

Companions

I N MAY 1978 ANNE HAS HAD ENOUGH. She leaves the newspaper office. She applies for a doctorate at the Humboldt University. Historical research strikes her as a protected area. Today she says it was an escape from reality. The subject of her thesis is the history of the Spanish trade-union movement. She didn't choose the subject herself, but it strikes her as innocuous enough. She doesn't want to have any more aggravation. Anne is working in the library of the Institute for Marxism–Leninism. At some point she orders a book which the librarian tells her can only be borrowed with a special permit. Anne learns that there's a whole department in the library containing works banned in the GDR. Anne's tutor procures the permit, and one winter afternoon in 1979 Anne is allowed for the first time to enter the "poison room" in which the dangerous books are catalogued. To her surprise the banned books aren't by bourgeois historians, but all by left-wing dissenters. The whole of Trotskyite literature is collected here, along with the works of theorists of the labour movement decried by the Party as "Eurocommunists", "appeasers" and "revisionists". These are the books the Party is most afraid of, the ones to which they are most vehemently opposed. This secret library is a kind of traitors' crypt.

Anyone with access to the "poison room" can order whatever they like. No one checks whether the borrowed books are connected with the academic project on which the person ordering the book is working. Anne orders whatever she can get her hands on. Books by renegades, by apostates she had only known by name, are suddenly on the table in front of her. And because work on her doctorate is progressing far too quickly anyway, or so her colleagues think, she uses the time to fill herself up with forbidden knowledge. She reads Trotsky, Bukharin and Solzhenitsyn. A whole cosmos of ideas and thoughts opens itself up to her. She finds questions that she's often asked herself, and answers that leave her speechless because they're so different to the ones she's grown up with. She understands that the certainties and dogmas she's been dealing with until then are only one possible interpretation of Marxism–Leninism. That there is an unlimited number of possible ways of thinking about Socialism. The proscribed theorists who often had to pay with their lives for their thoughts strike her as much more honest and courageous than the ideologists of "really existing Socialism". For them, Socialism is not the dictatorship of a party but the dreamlike vision of a new society in which freedom and Socialism are not a contradiction. With every book she reads, she becomes increasingly convinced that the GDR is actually preventing Socialism, instead betraying and perverting it. For Anne this is at once a relief and a burden because she knows that she believes in the right cause, but unfortunately lives in the wrong country.

Anne knows that there is a proscribed writer in her own family, branded a "'right-wing traitor" in the official history of the GDR. It's her grandfather Dagobert Lubinski, her mother's father. Dagobert was a Jewish Communist who lived in Düsseldorf and worked as an economic journalist for the Party newspaper *Freiheit*. In 1928 he was excluded from the KPD along with others because he openly stood up to the policy of the Party. Her grandfather is not mentioned much in the family. There is a photograph of him in the big bookshelf in the sitting room. The photograph shows a bald man with round nickel glasses and a cigarette in the corner of his mouth, looking confidently past the camera. Every now and again Anne learns a few scraps about him that she has to assemble herself. She knows that in 1943 Dagobert was murdered in Auschwitz by the Nazis, and that he had been in prison in Düsseldorf for a long time before that. She knows he founded a group in 1928, called the "Kommunistische Partei Opposition", KPO for short. In the East German history books they talk about a "splinter group" that went over "to the camp of the class enemies". They speak of "hostile machinations of dissenting appeasers", after whose disempowerment and exposure a new chapter in Party history could begin—the time of unity and solidarity, which Anne had learnt of as a historical advance.

When Anne's mother talks about Dagobert, she soon has tears in her eyes. Gerhard prefers not to talk about Dagobert at all. His painful story is like a dark, mysterious stain on the family chronicle. Anne feels magically attracted to her grandfather. She feels a connection with this strange man, and she is unable to explain it. Again and again she decides to take a serious look into his history. And again and again she drops the idea. It's as if she senses that Dagobert will change her life.

In the early Eighties, Anne's mother gives her the letters that Dagobert wrote from prison in Düsseldorf. The letters are Dagobert's legacy, in which he formulates his final thoughts. "Keep the letters!" he writes again and again. Perhaps he already knows that apart from a photograph they will be the only thing that remains of him.

Anne learns that the KPO produced a magazine called *Against the Stream*. She looks for it in the catalogue of forbidden books, but finds nothing. Anne asks the librarian, and it turns out that there is a locked catalogue for which even the "poison room" isn't secure enough. This catalogue is in the office of the library director, and very special permission is required to access it. It takes another few months, and a certain amount of persuasion, before Anne receives the requisite permission. The librarian who finally brings the dusty volumes to her seat says that no one has ordered this title for a very long time. Anne flicks through the first edition, published at the end of 1928. There is only text, no pictures, and every now and again a framed appeal to the readers to donate money so that the magazine can appear again. The motto of the magazine is: "He who wants to get back to the spring must swim against the stream." Anne likes that sentence very much.

She looks for Dagobert's name in the register, but doesn't find it. The most-named author in the economics section is Erich Lessing, often abbreviated to E.L. Once next to his name there is the reference: our economics expert from Düsseldorf. Did Dagobert write under a pseudonym? Anne orders a volume of the Düsseldorf KPD paper *Freiheit*, for which Dagobert wrote until he was thrown out of the Party. Almost all the articles on economics are signed E.L. So it is him.

From the magazines Anne learns a lot about her grandfather's history. The split between Dagobert and the KPD was caused by the decision of the Communist International in August 1928 to declare Social Democracy to be the main enemy of the Communist movement. The Social Democrats were at least as bad and dangerous as the fascists, it said in the paper that was delivered at a congress in Moscow. The Communist workers were told to leave their trade unions and form their own "revolutionary associations". Dagobert was at the congress in Moscow. Later, in an article, he described the Party's decision as "a policy bordering on insanity", because it split the working class and thus paved the way for the Nazis. Many other comrades saw it the same way, hundreds were thrown out of the Party because they persisted in their dissenting opinions. The leading men of the opposition were called Heinrich Brandler and August Thalheimer. Both worked at KPD headquarters in the early Twenties, and were fired by Moscow for incorrect behaviour. They assumed that the majority of workers followed the SPD and the trade unions, and that it was therefore important to act together. Until 1928 such views were tolerated in the Party, but after the Moscow congress there was a switch of direction, called the "Bolshevization" of the Party, which meant nothing but the complete elimination of democracy within the Party. Until then, Anne learns in these old magazines, there had always been violent debates within the Party. The various factions argued with each other, but no one was demonized as an enemy. The representatives of the minority, she reads with astonishment in an article, were even given extra time to speak to set out their concerns in detail.

Anne is astonished that this form of democracy had ever existed in the Party. She only knows the compulsion to unanimity. In her experience opposition amounts to hostility. Dagobert had known the old Party, so he and his fellow campaigners had vehemently put forward their opinions until the end. In October 1928 Dagobert is fired from the editorial team of *Freiheit*. A month later a campaign is waged in the same paper "against the Brandler-Thalheimer faction under the leadership of the Comrades Becker, Rautenbach, Lubinski and Strobl". Anne reads the articles that accompany the fall of her grandfather. In December and January the tone hardens.

Now there is no mention of comrades. They are called "right-wing liquidators", who are "waging an underground war of subversion with poisoned weapons". On 8 January 1929 Dagobert is "excluded from the Communist Party on the grounds of his continued factional work against the Party", as *Freiheit* announces in bold type. This is, incidentally, the same newspaper in which Gerhard will take his first steps as a journalist after the war.

This tone, this vehemence, with which "the enemies of the working class" are published in the Party press, is familiar to Anne. It's the same language, the same hate-filled destructive rhetoric that she herself encountered in newspaper editorial offices in the GDR. Except here a member of her own family was suddenly in the stocks. Someone she knew was not an enemy. Someone who had even been proved right only a few years later when the KPD's strategy in fact turned out to be a disaster. With their narrow-minded policy against the Social Democrats, the German Communists decisively encouraged the rise of Adolf Hitler. They made themselves partially guilty. That this error was later acknowledged and recognized did not, however, mean that the people who had tried to prevent that mistake from the outset were in any way rehabilitated. Anne remembered a seminar about the history of the German labour movement in which the professor explained that the KPO had been wrong in spite of everything, because they had opposed the decisions of the Party. This lack of discipline was a graver crime than anything else.

Anne can't shake off her grandfather. For her, he is proof that one can be right and on the other side. That the supposed traitors are sometimes the better comrades. Dagobert frees her of her fear of becoming a traitor herself. Dagobert becomes a key for her, which will allow her to escape the "prison of loyalty". That is what she calls that profound feeling that has for so long bound her to the state. The feeling that she must not harm the GDR because it is the safe haven that offers peace and protection to her persecuted parents.

Today Anne says that she identified with her parents in their persecution. That was the core of her dependency. And now all of a sudden there was someone else who also belonged to her family, who was also persecuted, who was also a good Communist and who still followed his own convictions. A man with a heroic tale very different to that of her father. With this other hero, she sensed, she might be able to break that old dependency and finally become free. The things that had inhibited her until now—history and the family—could now help her find her own way.

At six o'clock in the morning on 3 November 1936, Dagobert is arrested by the Gestapo at his apartment in Düsseldorf. He is accused of belonging to an illegal Communist group. The last testimony that Anne has of him is the death certificate issued in April 1943 by the register office of Auschwitz II. It testified "that the journalist Dagobert Israel Lubinski died on 22 February 1943 at 6.45 in Auschwitz, Kasernenstrasse".

Dagobert was deported to Auschwitz not because of his political work, but because he was a Jew. When Anne starts becoming interested in his story, she also comes across Dagobert's family, which lived in Breslau, Prague and Hamburg, and which she finds again in autumn 1941, in the Litzmannstadt Ghetto. In May 1942 they ended up on the first transportation to Chełmno extermination camp, where they were all killed in gas trucks. Anne is shattered to discover this, because the story she was most familiar with was the one about her father's Jewish relations, most of whom were able to escape to safety. Dagobert's wife Charlotte survived because she was Aryan, and their two daughters, Nora and Hannah, just escaped deportation as "mixed blood, first degree". It is only now that Anne learns of the fear in which her mother Nora lived for months because she was on the deportation list in autumn 1944, and didn't know whether they would come and get her. The owner of a clay quarry in the Westerwald had hidden Nora at his house. He offered to leave her at the clay quarry and provide her with food if this proved necessary. A day after the Americans marched into the Westerwald, the man wanted written confirmation for his help. The man was a member of the Nazi Party and the SA. Saving a half-Jew may well have spared him serious unpleasantness.

For the first time Anne feels part of a Jewish family. It's a funny feeling. As a historian she is used to remaining detached from events, but now history has caught up with her. She doesn't know where she fits in this family. She somehow belongs to it, but she also finds it presumptuous to place herself in a line with the dead. Her parents have repressed their Jewish heritage, and even Dagobert, her new hero, didn't want to have anything to do with it. Assimilation, he is supposed to have said to his daughters, was the only way forward for the Jews in Germany. Anne goes to the Library of the Jewish Community and starts reading. She tries to achieve an objective view of the matter, she finds the feelings too strange. But rather than emerging from the pull of the emotions, she is drawn deeper and deeper into them. In the community she meets other children of survivors. She understands that you can't just push all those things away, that it's too late for an objective and detached perspective. She's in the midst of her own story. Sometimes somebody in the community asks if she doesn't want to become a member. She says she's in the process of freeing herself from another community of faith. "That's quite enough for one life."

I remember meeting Anne in the street in Karlshorst one day. I must have been about fifteen. When she saw me, she started crying. We hugged and she told me the son of Augustin the baker had called my brother a "stupid Jew" at school. I had no idea how the son of Augustin the baker had worked out that we might be Jews. Anne didn't know either. But she was very troubled by it. A few weeks later she read to my brother's class from the memoirs of a Jewish prisoner who had survived Auschwitz. There was no trouble after that. It was also the time when I started thinking about what it meant to me to come from a Jewish family. My mother had told me that the Jews had always been a very disillusioned people, which was why Jewish descent was always passed down through the mother and not through the father, because you could never be sure if he really was the father. Because in their family only both grandfathers were Jewish, I couldn't have been left with much. In the book that Anne would later write about her grandfather, she writes on the question of what it means to be Jewish: "Perhaps the feeling of a stigma, the thought of the dead, of the survivors scattered all over the world, and a slightly strange feeling about myself." I think it's a great description.

In March 1982 Anne has a *Parteiüberprüfungsgespräch*, a "scrutinizing conversation", a kind of confession for loyal comrades. She stands in a seminar room in the main building of the Humboldt University.

Sitting facing her are three comrades from the Party leadership. This time Anne decides to say everything. She has decided to accept expulsion from the Party if there's no way of preventing it. Anne talks about all the things she doesn't agree with. The lies, the rigid thinking, the ideology that ended up deep-frozen at some point. She says she has profound doubts. She listens to herself, chasing after the words pouring from her mouth, apparently beyond her control. She thinks something bad is about to happen to her. But nothing happens. The comrades smile at her benignly, saying that everyone has their doubts and problems. The only important thing is that she remains a Socialist deep down. It seems that things have changed somewhat. The Party has become softer. And it's clear that nobody is being thrown out of the Party any more. She would have to take that step herself. But Anne doesn't think about that at all. She is relieved to be able to keep her opinion and still remain a comrade.

After she's finished her doctoral thesis, Anne receives an offer to work for a magazine called the *Neue Berliner Illustrierte*. She doesn't actually want to work in journalism in the GDR any more, but on the other hand she has to do something. She decides to give it another try. But it quickly becomes apparent that she can't do it any more, she's emotionally too remote from it. In the spring of 1986 she is to write an article about the Marx-Engels monument that has been erected near the Berlin television tower. She thinks the monument is ugly and the sculptor dreadful. She scribbles something together, and the few aspects that seem interesting to her are deleted too, and even the title is changed. "The memorial to the working class", it says above her text. When she leaves the office in the evening she knows she has reached the limit of her compromises. She resigns and stays at home the next day. She can't do it any more.

In the flat in Karlshorst there is a lovely veranda with big windows on all sides. There are old lime trees outside the windows. This veranda is where Anne now wants to work. Wolf makes shelves and a desk out of old floorboards. He's glad that Anne is finally working at home too, as he had always advised. "Do you feel this freedom?" he asks, and she cries because she feels so lost. She knows she is outside once and for all, that there's no going back. She is thrown back on her own devices, alone in her little world. Of course she can do what she wants now, but what does she actually want? It's a while before she decides to write a book about Dagobert. After all, it's partly his fault that she can no longer function out there. The photograph from her parents' bookshelf is now on her desk. Her ostracized grandfather has become her new companion.

21

Declarations of Faith

T WO WEEKS AFTER WOLF YELLED at my headmistress Frau Reichenbach over the business with the sub-machine gun, we got news that my application to sit the Abitur had been turned down, which made Wolf very sad because he now really thought it was all his fault. In a letter from the district school council it said, "Among the applicants many pupils have a much higher capacity for achievement, along with model behaviour." In general, only the two best from each class were allowed to go on to extended secondary school. At our school they were Christiane and Sven, who were really better than me. In Russian and maths I had only a Three, and my work was assessed as "inadequate". Even so, Anne objected. She said she could not allow this state to make a worker out of her son. Anne wrote to the school council to say she would complain to Erich Honecker if I wasn't allowed to do the Abitur. But the school council wasn't particularly impressed. The rejection stood, and I asked my mother not to write to Erich Honecker, because I suspected that the General Secretary might have more important things to do than worry about a school place for me.

The business with the Abitur was difficult for all of us. I didn't know what to do after school, it was becoming clear to Anne that the country was not good for her children, and Wolf still thought everything was his fault. For the first time I felt the power of this state, which could simply determine what path one's life could take. And I thought for the first time about what path mine might be. Everything until then had been clear and straightforward, but suddenly there were decisions to be made.

Anyone who didn't do the Abitur had to learn a trade at sixteen. Just doing nothing wasn't an option in the GDR. I actually wanted to be a chemist, because I enjoyed chemistry and it had nothing to do with politics. But it's also possible that I was interested in it because my friend Sven wanted to be a chemist as well. Anne and Wolf made enquiries and found me an apprenticeship as a chemistry-lab assistant in the Academy of Sciences. The plan was later to let me switch from work to study. But first of all I had to do that training. The practical part took place at VEB Berlin-Chemie in Adlershof. It started at seven in the morning, which meant that I had to leave at six. The tram that ran from Karlshorst to Schöneweide was so full at that time of day that you had to force your way in. I had had no idea until then that so many people were out and about so early in the morning. Most of them were workers going to the Oberspree cable works. Their faces were pale, their eyes stared into the distance. Some even managed to sleep standing up. After a year I could do the same. It was worst in winter when it was still dark in the morning. The walk from the factory gates to the production hall was not without its hazards. Foul-smelling gas hissed from rusty pipes, little streams of corrosive liquid flowed along the paths. When insulin for diabetics was being manufactured it smelt of decomposing pig placenta. Our foreman insisted on punctuality, and because I generally didn't get to work on time I usually had to scour the big mixing pot by way of punishment.

This switch from pampered childhood to reality in the GDR was a shock to me. I felt lost, like a fish out of water. I thought of the others who were now allowed to sit the Abitur, of the heated, clean classrooms, the books, and the pride they must feel at being among the best. I saw my colleagues in their grey padded cotton jackets, the trees white with chalk dust, the pall of smoke that hung over the factory. This reality seemed terribly unreal to me, exaggeratedly wretched and bad. I didn't want to work in this factory, I didn't want to be a chemist any more, I just wanted to get away. I was like a spoilt child that has to take his first steps on his own and immediately starts to stumble. All of a sudden I understood how little my parents' world had to do with everything else that was happening in the country. How shielded from reality I had been in that airy, warm household of intellectuals. I understood now why it was so important for my father to work at home, to be independent, why my mother wanted at all costs to stop them turning me into a worker. My parents' friends were photographers, painters, designers, architects or doctors. They all lived far from the everyday life of the GDR, far from the toiling masses who kept this country running. I felt like an exile, like someone banished to reality.

Vocational school wasn't as I'd imagined it either. Our citizenship teacher Herr Thumm, a massive, bearded man who also taught sport, thought it was important to have a solid class perspective. It wasn't enough for him that we should learn the nonsense he told us off by heart. He demanded declarations of faith, and if someone's voice failed them he would have a hard time at school because Herr Thumm was also a Party secretary and none of my fellow students dared to contradict him. Herr Thumm quickly marked me out as an enemy, because I had once admitted to watching Western television for the sake of information. He involved me in discussions which he guided so skilfully that eventually I had no option but to reveal my true, traitorous thoughts. Then he would nod triumphantly like a policeman who has just caught a thief *in flagrante*. His eyes narrowed to little slits, and he told me he would cut me down to size sooner or later. "This size with a hat on," he said, pointing at his fleshy thumbs. Even today I sometimes think of those conversations, and imagine I could still have them and throw my steely arguments right into his beardy face. In my imagination Herr Thumm is finally sitting there speechless, unable to escape my reasoning. In those days it was more often the case that I was left sitting there in silence, fighting back the tears. He managed to scare me. And I did become a little smaller.

Anne advised me to do the Abitur at evening class. You could only do that if you already had a job. Apprentices were also accepted in unusual cases. The headmistress of Treptow technical college asked me how I planned to do both things at the same time. Vocational school and Abitur. "You won't stand the pace," she said. But I wanted at least to try. My apprenticeship lasted from seven till four. The Abitur classes ran from five till ten. Quite honestly, even today I don't know how I managed to do that for three years. I wanted to get back to my old world at all costs. And I could only do that with the Abitur.

On my first day at technical college, this was in the spring of 1987, the classroom was so full that there weren't enough tables for everybody. The physics teacher told us not to worry because in a month at most everyone would have a desk of their own. And so indeed they did. Our numbers dwindled by the week, until only fifteen students remained. Our citizenship teacher was called Ecki, and he insisted that that was what we called him. Ecki had a beard, small, calm eyes, and wore sandals with thick woollen socks. In our first class he wrote a quotation from Heine on the board: "We need a united Germany, united both inside and out." We spent a whole class talking about that sentence, which seemed so dangerous to me that I didn't dare copy it into my notebook. Until that point I had never thought about whether there might ever be a reunification. That would have meant the GDR somehow disappearing, and I couldn't imagine that. Ecki explained that in philosophy it was important to think the unthinkable, because otherwise you always remained stuck in the present. "So let's be philosophers for a while and wonder what might come after the GDR." We were electrified, because none of us had ever experienced a citizenship class like that. Ecki drew a table on the board. We were to tell him the pros and cons of the GDR that occurred to us in the course of a minute. Strangely, at that moment all I could think of were the pros, because we'd always learnt them off by heart. The others seemed to feel the same. The second column was left blank. "'Seems to be a perfect country," said Ecki and wrote in the cons column, "Students don't dare to say what they think." That was too much for us, and a long recital of shortcomings began. No freedom of opinion, no freedom of travel, too little fruit, no free elections, no decent jeans, no press freedom. As far as I remember those were the main points. We sat there, excited, faces glowing, it was the first time that we were able to say something in school that we really thought.

The other teachers at the technical college were also unlike the teachers we'd had until then. It turned out that some of them were no longer allowed to teach at secondary schools and were therefore employed on a freelance basis. Our German teacher, Frau Bietz, brought in books by Bulgakov and read to us from them. Our Russian teacher regretted the fact that none of us wanted to speak Russian, but she sympathized, and left us alone in the classroom during tests so that we could copy things down from our cribs in peace. After two years there were only eight of us. The fewer of us there were, the tighter we were as a group. We met at the weekend and did our homework together. I gave private coaching in chemistry and German, and received support in maths and Russian in return. My fellow pupils were rather jolly characters. One of them worked as a janitor in a children's home and wanted to study music. Another was a seamstress in a theatre and planned to become a textile designer. Each of us had fallen through the net of the GDR school system at some point, and each of us still had aspirations.

Just before Christmas 1986 Gerhard asked me if I fancied going to France with him in the summer. He said he wanted to show all his grandchildren the places where he had fought in the Resistance, and as the oldest I would be the first. I was so amazed that I couldn't think of anything to say at first. The idea of a sixteen-year-old being allowed to go on a trip to the West was about as likely as Erich Honecker with a punk hairdo. Gerhard said someone he knew in the Politburo would sort out the permit. In the meantime I should mug up on my French so that he didn't need to feel ashamed of me. A month later I was summoned to police headquarters on Alexanderplatz. On the ground floor people stood in long queues to make their travel applications. Gerhard had told me to take the lift to the second floor because there was a special travel desk there. On the second floor the corridors were wood-panelled and there were no queues. The only person sitting in the waiting room was Frank Schöbel, a GDR singing star, who clearly had good connections as well. After a short wait I was called in and a friendly policewoman in a red uniform asked me to sign my passport. The policewoman asked me how long I planned to stay in France and which border crossing was going to be most convenient. It seemed to be the most normal thing in the world to want to spend your summer in France. Ten minutes later I was back in the lift, holding a blue passport and an exit visa. I should have been yelling with joy, but I felt somehow paralysed. It was all so unreal, this waiting room, this friendly policewoman. How could it suddenly be so easy to get over that stupid border? Gerhard had opened the Wall for me with a phone call.

The Politburo informed my vocational school about my impending trip to France. I was summoned to see the headmistress, who was quite upset, and granted me two weeks' extra holiday. The best thing was the look on the face of Herr Thumm, the citizenship teacher, who no longer understood the world. Why was someone like me allowed to travel to the West? He tried not to show it, but it was clear that Herr Thumm, possibly for the first time in his life, doubted a decision by the Politburo.

We set off early in July, in Gerhard's light-brown Citroën Pallas GDA. The closer we get to the border in Marienborn, the emptier the autobahn gets. There's a sign saying that this is the last exit in the GDR. We drive on, there are no more Eastern cars, even though we are in the East. At a walking pace we drive past the barbed-wire fences and anti-tank barriers, the soldiers with sub-machine guns and the chevaux de frise. Gerhard tunes the car radio to a classical-music station and hums along. He never usually does that. Perhaps he's embarrassed for me to see how barricaded our country is. What became of a dream of Socialism.

A border guard checks our passports, and then we're allowed to drive on. I ask Gerhard if we're in the West now, and he asks if I can't smell it, because the air here is quite different from the air at home. He laughs. I think it's the first time I've ever heard him make a joke about the GDR.

First of all we drive to see Aunt Hannah in Düsseldorf, the city where Anne was born. Hannah gives me fifty Western marks, and I walk around the streets a little, buy a pack of Camels and feel fantastic. The next day we travel on via Aachen to Brussels. I'm amazed that there are no checks at the border into Belgium. Gerhard tells me about how he escaped across the border with his parents near Aachen. I listen to what he says, but I'm actually far too busy absorbing all the new things. The colours, the smells, the cars. In Brussels we eat mussels and chips, and Gerhard tells me he ate mussels with his parents back then as well.

It's only clear to me now that this trip was a historical forensic investigation. That it wasn't about the West, it was about Gerhard's story. It could be that he was a bit disappointed by me, because in those days I was much less interested in the past than in the present. I didn't care that much about the Third Reich. I was in the West for the first time, and that was what mattered.

Later, when we arrive in France, Gerhard turns into a different person. All of a sudden he is relaxed and witty. He talks nineteen to the dozen and seems strangely rejuvenated. He seems much happier there than in the GDR.

I didn't think much more about it at the time, but today I believe he felt really at home in France. In the country of his youth, surrounded by the old stories and adventures, by the time when the historical truth was still so simple. It was certainly no coincidence that he repeatedly lived abroad, that he always wanted to get away. Even though he convinced himself that the East German state was anti-fascist and historically superior, he also knew that there were people living in the GDR who had cheered Hitler on. And did he

In France, 1987

not find the uniformity of thought in the GDR somehow familiar? Didn't he find it a bit strange when the FDJ marched along Stalinallee with flaming torches?

The boundless hatred of Israel in East German propaganda can't have left him cold either. In Gerhard's Stasi file there's a memo from June 1967 reporting on an event in East German television. At the time Gerhard presented a foreign-policy magazine programme called *Objektiv*, broadcast once a month. The Stasi note says: "An article was prepared for today's *Objektiv* programme which was supposed to expose the background of the aggressive state of Israel as an outpost of global imperialism in the Arab world which is systematically developing its functions on behalf of the oil monopolies. Comrade Leo declared that it couldn't be done like that. He refused to voice this article for the broadcast, saying it was anti-Semitic. As is well known, Gerhard Leo is of Jewish descent, and is even supposed to have relatives in Israel. The episode of *Objektiv* broadcast by DFF on 15.6.67 was cancelled, and instead extracts from the election rally were shown with Comrade Walter Ulbricht in Leipzig, in which Israel's aggressive policy was mentioned. The cancellation of the *Objektiv* programme is a hitherto unique and incomparable event. Leo was immediately relieved of his function in television broadcasting."

Had this matter suddenly prompted him to stand up as a Jew again? He, who would have liked nothing better than to shed all that, had to side with Israel because no one else did. Because anti-Semitism bothered no one but him. He, the Jew, was punished because he couldn't stand anti-Semitism. He'd probably repressed it all, but he certainly hadn't forgotten it. I imagine his relationship with the GDR at this point as being something like a marriage of convenience. But his beloved lives in France.

That beloved casts a spell over him in the weeks we spend driving through the land of his youth. We drink champagne with his Resistance comrades in Corrèze, and when Gerhard is tipsy he sings the old songs with them. He tells stories of beautiful women and drinking sprees, and when we are standing at Allassac station, where he was liberated by the partisans, tears run down his cheeks. All of a sudden he is so human, so vulnerable. And so happy. In a restaurant in the old port of Marseilles he orders oysters and white wine. He says I've learnt in school that capitalism is about to die out. Then he pauses and smiles. "You have to admit, it's a beautiful death." I don't recognize my grandfather any more. At home I had the feeling he had a steel band around his chest. Here he sits in the sun grinning like a schoolboy.

We also go to see his friend Gilles Perrault, who is a famous writer in France and has a country house near Avignon, which even has a swimming pool. There are also other guests in the house, which is surrounded by vineyards. For example Régis Debray, a small, round man who tells us over dinner how he fought with Che Guevara in Bolivia. He also tells us about Tamara Bunke, a woman from the GDR who was with Che in those days. "A remarkable woman, a fighter," he says. I don't understand everything, because my French isn't particularly good. But what I understand is that everybody in the house thinks the GDR is just brilliant. Gilles Perrault says I can be proud to live in such a revolutionary country, because only revolutions really liberate people. I don't dare to contradict him, not least because I see how happy these words are making Gerhard. But I don't get it. How can you sit in a villa like that and rave about the GDR? Or do you have to sit in a villa like this one to be able to? I don't know what image these people have of the GDR, or whether they've ever even been there. Régis Debray confides a secret. He is working as a foreign-policy adviser to the French President François Mitterrand, and he says Mitterrand is a big fan of the GDR. "If the GDR didn't exist, Germany would be far too big," says Debray. And Gilles Perrault remembers a quote from the author François Mauriac, who once said he loved Germany so much that he was glad there were two of them. The men laugh and clink glasses, and I reflect that it's a very pleasant business, being a revolutionary in the South of France.

On our journey back to the revolutionary GDR I travel on alone from Düsseldorf by train. That means I can stop off in West Berlin. I want to see the Wall, which is the highlight of this trip. Seeing the Wall from the other side, just once. I spend the whole day walking along the border, I touch the cool concrete, which is colourfully painted on the Western side. I climb up viewing towers and look across. For hours. I see the neatly raked death strip, the border guards standing in their watchtowers looking through binoculars. The dome of the television tower gleams in the sunlight. Everything's so close and yet so far away.

Five or six times I take the S-Bahn back and forth between Lehrter Bahnhof and Friedrichstrasse. Friedrichstrasse station is in the East, but if you stay on the platform you can travel back to the West. I can't get enough of that weird feeling of travelling to the East and coming straight back out again. It's exciting and oppressive, confusing and cheering, brilliant and sad. I feel my heart beating faster every time the S-Bahn crosses the Spree Bridge, past the Reichstag, on which the huge black, red and gold flag flies. I'm not sure which journey I prefer. The one to the East, to the prison that is my home, or the one to the West, into alien freedom. I think what it would be like not to go back and simply stay in the West. I could do that now, no one would stop me. Perhaps I'd have to spend a few months in a children's home until I reach adulthood. But I could do a Western Abitur and have a Western girlfriend. If I go back I'll be stuck again. On the other hand, what am I going to do all on my own in the West? As a refugee I can't go home, and my family wouldn't be able to go anywhere either. And Gerhard would be really annoyed, and so would Anne and Wolf. Is it worth it? I don't know.

Just before midnight, a few minutes before my visa runs out, I go back to Friedrichstrasse station. There's no turning back this time. I walk down the long, tiled corridors in which tramps from the West sit with their dogs. They drink from big schnapps bottles that they buy in the GDR Intershops at the station because alcohol is cheaper here than in the West. I push my passport under a pane of glass, a border guard looks at me intently. The stamp thuds on the paper and I go on to the metal door that only has a handle on the inside. The door slams behind me like a mousetrap. I'm home again.

Of course it was the right decision, precisely because I'm home again. On the other hand I now knew that I wanted to go to the West as soon as I was old enough, to find a new home. It wasn't just an idea, but a plan I firmly believed in.

When I tell Anne and Wolf about it one evening after dinner, a sudden silence falls at our table. Perhaps they can sense how serious I am. That at some point I would be prepared to leave them. Anne says she herself would never go to the West, whatever happened in the East. But she understands me, she says, she just doesn't want me doing anything rash, because I still have time. Wolf talks about how he himself once stood by the barbed-wire fence in Teltow. It's the first time he's talked to me about it. He talks about his mother, whom he didn't want to leave alone, and I don't know whether that's supposed to be a request not to go.

I can't talk to Gerhard about things like that. He probably didn't even guess what that trip to France had sparked in me. He wanted to show me the sites of his struggle, and I was busy betraying his GDR. But what did he think I would do? Or couldn't he imagine someone who had grown up in the East wanting eventually to go to the West?

After my return, the GDR strikes me as even more wretched than before. For a few days I see the East the way Westerners have probably always seen it. It's as if someone had suddenly taken the colour out of the world. Even the photographs of France that I hand in to be developed at the stationery shop in Karlshorst look somehow bleached on the East German paper. I find everything stupid and ugly, and I quite enjoy playing the part of the global traveller, letting the hicks back home feel a little of my contempt. The only problem is that it doesn't get better. I can't find my way out of the role I'm playing. I refuse to be normal again. Perhaps because it would feel like a setback, a defeat.

It's now—I was seventeen—that this strange game begins. This game in which dream and reality mingle until I myself can't disentangle them. Because I'm no longer just dreaming of the West, I'm acting as if I'm already a Westerner. A Westerner in the East. It starts with a Falk street map that I brought back from West Berlin. A few months after my return I'm giving an acquaintance from Munich a guided tour of East Berlin. I'm holding this colourful street map in my hand, and it strikes me that people are looking at me in a quite different way than usual. They clearly think I'm a Western tourist. It's a great feeling. The way these Easterners look at me from the corner of their eyes, as if they're watching curiously after me, makes me happy.

But I'm not sure it hasn't got something to do with the real Westerner I'm with. So I ask two mates from vocational school if they fancy being Westerners for an afternoon. One of them still has a copy of the *Frankfurter Allgemeine Zeitung* that an aunt brought him years ago. We all wear Western jeans, which makes things considerably easier. And then, street map and newspaper in hand, we stroll to the Brandenburg Gate and talk loudly about how the border looks completely different from the other side. And immediately they're there again, those looks. We visit the French Cathedral and ask directions from locals. I speak West German all the time, meaning without Berlin dialect and slightly more loudly than usual. I also sometimes say "*gelle?*" at the end of sentences, because I've heard that in the

West. In the Operncafé we ask if we can pay in Western marks. This is followed by some jostling among the waiters, because they all want to serve us. And in the end there's a lot of disappointment because all we can find is a few Eastern marks, "from the compulsory money exchange," as we tell them.

We take our game further and further. Once a week we have our Western day. We go to Sanssouci and the Jewish cemetery in Weissensee, we climb the television tower and go to the Pergamon Museum. The things Westerners do in the East. Each of us has come up with a Western biography so that we don't get muddled in our conversations with Easterners. My mother is a journalist with *Stern*, my father has a gallery in Charlottenburg. I'm currently doing my Abitur at a humanist *Gymnasium* in Steglitz. Intensive Latin course, no one in the East can speak it anyway. My family belong to the left-wing bourgeoisie. Flat in an old apartment with double doors, holidays in France, skiing in Austria.

We tell our Easterner acquaintances about our life in the West, about that elegant, relaxed society where everyone makes his own decisions about what he does. Our West is a country where the people are well dressed, drive comfortable cars, where everything smells like it does in Intershop. The complete opposite of grey squalor, the anti-GDR. Probably only a fake Westerner can rave about the West like that to an Easterner. We know the yearnings of the Easterners very well, they're our own. The more stories we tell, the deeper we plunge into our dream world.

Chatting up East German women is no longer a problem for us. It never goes particularly far, however, because we have to be "back on the other side" by midnight. Once two women from Jena walk us to the so-called "Hall of Tears" at Friedrichstrasse station. And there really are tears. We join the exit queue, ask the women to go and make leaving easier, then creep secretly away. We feel a bit mean after that. We drop the game, and for the first time I think seriously about leaving the country.

At this time, in spring 1988, practically everyone I know is thinking more or less seriously about how to get out as quickly and elegantly as possible. There isn't a party at which the subject doesn't come up at some point. People talk about other people who have just managed it or are still trying. Two friends of mine want to marry Western men so that they can get out, others are waiting for their Western grandma's seventieth birthday to try their luck. There are people who go and work for the Permanent Representation of the Federal Republic in East Berlin before having themselves quietly transferred to the West. Word has it that there are bedrooms for East German refugees in the West German Embassy in Prague. People who have an official exit application being processed tie white ribbons to their car aerials. They're all disappearing, one after another. And the ones who stay behind feel like failures. "Der Doofe Rest"—the stupid leftovers—is what the GDR was called at the time. For the time being I'm happy to deal with the question of emigrating, of keeping that thought moving in my head. When I think about it I get a pleasant tingly feeling in my stomach.

It's also the case that the East is getting really interesting again around about now. All of a sudden there are great bands I've never heard of, they only play music from the West in the clubs, and there are all kinds of wild parties. It all had to do with the end-times vibe that prevailed, at least in Prenzlauer Berg. People are partying as if it were the last time. People are living for the moment because the future isn't going to bring anything anyway. I remember a fashion show in the old swimming pool on Oderberger Strasse. A group of designers put on a weird and beautiful show, followed by dancing in the empty swimming pool. An acquaintance of mine had good contacts with the West, so he always had a decent amount of hash in the house. He's squatting in a huge flat on Marienburger Strasse, and there are parties there once a week. The Pink Floyd film *The Wall* is showing on a television screen, and we lie in front of it smoking and kissing. There are always a few diplomats' kids from the Permanent Representation. Once the son of the British ambassador brings his parents along when we're having a party on the roof. The ambassador is pretty impressed when he sees all the frenzied activity, because it doesn't fit with his image of the GDR.

But eventually even these parties lose their charm. They're an opportunity to forget the rest for a few hours. But when the rush passes, the rest is still there. And the more excessive the parties, the bigger the comedown. At one of these parties I meet an actress who's married an Austrian and has two passports because the GDR allows dual nationality if you marry an Austrian. She lives in East Berlin and can travel to the West whenever she likes. That strikes me as the perfect way of combining Western freedom and familiar security. Also, Gerhard's sister lives in Vienna, and I'm pretty sure they could find a distant cousin who'd be willing to marry me. The actress advises me to go to the lawyer Lothar de Maizière, who had also acted as intermediary in her wedding. A week later, in March 1989, I'm sitting in a lawyer's office on Chausseestrasse in front of the desk of a man who a year later would be the first freely elected Prime Minister of the GDR. De Maizière stands at the window and listens to my plan. Then he asks, "Is it about love or a passport?" I'm not prepared for a question like that, and hem and haw. De Maizière says the whole thing will take at least two years, and the question is whether my problem might not solve itself in some other way. I don't understand what he means. De Maizière sits down behind his desk, smiles and says that dual nationality assumes the existence of two countries. In the case of Austria you probably didn't need to worry, but there were other states whose future wasn't quite so certain. "Save your marriage for a woman you really love, that's my advice," he says, and sends me away.

22

Feelings of Spring

IN OCTOBER 1986 Wolf goes to the South Seas. That is, he actually only goes to the City Library and borrows a few books. He wants to get as far away as possible, and the South Seas are the furthest place he can think of. It's supposed to be a fantasy trip, an adventure in his head. On this journey he wants to paint pictures and later perhaps have an exhibition. A display of longing, a little provocation, a bit of fun. For months he travels around, immerses himself in this other world, wraps himself up in stories. He dreams of bright blue water, of white lagoons, carved wooden boats and bare-bosomed women with flowers in their hair. His paintings show a South Sea that is probably much more beautiful than the real one could ever be. Wolf draws maps with travel routes, writes a log in which he records his most important experiences. His whole style changes, even the Sandman stories for television are suddenly playing out under palm trees. Wolf paints postcards showing strange plants and bright patterns. The cards even end up in the shops, under the title "Polynesia". At the same time Wolf also makes another grey postcard. Anne and he are sitting on the sofa, there's a little potted palm in front of them and the blind over the window is down.

Wolf says this game with the state and with himself actually got more and more interesting in the last years of the GDR. There were no clear rules any more, boundaries were blurred. Spaces and possibilities arose, and sometimes disappeared again. No one could tell what was still allowed and what was forbidden. You had to try things out. Wolf talks about an art weekend in the little town of Coswig near Dresden. A painter colleague from Berlin had hired the Culture House in Coswig on some pretext or other. And all of a sudden hundreds of people arrived from all over the country. For two days they make music, dance, paint, party. The police are too busy, the Stasi don't know a thing. A few months later there's a huge summer party on a farm in the Uckermark. The whole place is full of tents, there are barbecues and skinny-dipping, and bands play in the evening. There's a cabaret evening with Wolfgang Krause Zwieback, a fantastic word artist who isn't allowed to perform in the GDR, but that evening nobody's interested. The police turn up the next day and their names are all taken down, but there are no consequences. Wolf says they sometimes felt that all that was left was the facade of the state, with nothing behind it.

But then one day there's a man at the door of the flat in Karlshorst, saying that Wolf has to make his mind up which side he's on. The man requests an interview, but Wolf doesn't want to talk to the Stasi. When the upstairs neighbour comes downstairs, the man forces his way into the flat because he doesn't want to be seen. Wolf grabs him by the jacket and throws him down the stairs. And a short time later a white Wartburg is standing outside our house with four men in it watching us in silence. When the Wartburg drives away it's followed immediately by a grey Lada with four different men sitting in it. I had an astronomy kit at the time and watched the men with my telescope. The ones in the Lada are quite fat. They sit there for hours, all crammed together. They're plainly not allowed to get out.

A few days later Wolf stops finding this game at all funny. The fear that had disappeared is back.

At the same time, in March 1988, a decision is made in the Artists' Association to give Wolf Leo a passport and allow him to travel to West Berlin for three days a year. It isn't entirely clear whether there's a connection between the Stasi car outside the front door and the passport in his pocket. Do they want Wolf to stay in the West? Wolf doesn't care, he enjoys his days in West Berlin and he meets a painter there who calls himself Nil Ausländer and has a gallery on Savignyplatz. Nil is a rough-and-ready type, who deliberately acts proletarian. His gallery is hung with portraits of Jewish relatives who have never really existed. Wolf likes the idea of just inventing a new family. The two men take to each other, and Nil suggests that Wolf have an exhibition at his gallery. At first that sounds like a rather utopian idea. But the following year, when Wolf gets a new three-day visa for West Berlin, he decides just to do it. On 14 May 1989 he drives our light-brown Trabant 601 to the border crossing at Heinrich Heine Strasse. The car is crammed full of paintings and three-dimensional figures. On the roof-rack there's three-metre cardboard figure, the dancer, who is being allowed into the West for the first time. The GDR border guards are surprised by the unannounced art transport, but they let him through. Just like that. Nil is waiting on the other side of the border in his red VW Polo. They drive to Charlottenburg in convoy. When they stop at a junction the passers-by gaze in surprise after the cardboard car with the cardboard dancer.

In the evening, at the exhibition opening, the Charlottenburg bourgeoisie jostle their way past the art clutching glasses of red wine. Nil solemnly announces that this is the first private exhibition of an artist from the GDR in the West. The Charlottenburgers find it all new and exciting, and lots of them are keen to buy something. But

Wolf doesn't know if he is actually able to sell anything. He doesn't want to do anything wrong, so he decides to pass. Nil finds that silly but amusing.

Later in the night there's a party on a factory floor in Kreuzberg. A man offers Wolf a joint—he doesn't know what it is and keels over after a few drags. At about three in the morning he drags himself groggily to the border crossing at Heinrich Heine Strasse. But everything's already in darkness there. Wolf knocks on a door and shouts. It takes a while before a border guard opens up and lets him back into the East.

Increasingly often Anne visits the Jewish community, where she feels at ease. She's started finding the Party more sympathetic as well. Sometimes she goes to residents' association meetings in Karlshorst, where she meets pensioners who are also sitting at home and just want to chat for a while. For the first time she isn't afraid of these meetings. The Party is now a lot of friendly old men who want to help her out of her coat. It's as if the system has lost its power over her. The arm of the state doesn't reach all the way into her glazed veranda. Anne reads a piece by a woman poet, describing her withdrawal into herself. She compares that retreat to hibernation: "Outwardly dead, inwardly alive, the heart beats better. It is waiting for spring."

Anne thinks she can already sense the spring. She feels as if the whole country is getting mellower and more relaxed. There's a new travel law making it easier to visit relatives in the West. Anne travels to Düsseldorf, Hamburg, Vienna, Jerusalem. She writes freelance articles that are no longer simply cobbled together. One of those

Anne, 1988

articles appears in September 1988 in the arts magazine *Sonntag*. It's about the relationship between the founders of the GDR and their children. She describes the journey of the anti-fascist fighters who became the government after the war, without taking a break. "How could they bury their rancour when they emerged from the camps in 1945 and assumed responsibility for the people? How many of them could trust someone who hadn't shared their fate? Was their relationship with us, their children's generation, not that of strict fathers who only had our best interests at heart? Didn't they want, too often, to decide for us what those interests were?" These are questions that had been barely asked in public until now. Because they get to the nub, because they are directed at the old men who still bear responsibility.

But it could also be that for Anne this article is above all a conversation with her own father. A conversation that she can't have with him herself, because Gerhard won't allow it. Anne tries again and again to put something in motion, to get her father to open up. But these attempts normally end in discord. In October 1988 Anne and Wolf are together for the first time in a while, visiting Anne's parents. The mood is friendly but reserved, as they don't want to argue. But eventually it kicks off anyway. Gerhard says he thinks what's happening in the Soviet Union is a good thing, that glasnost and perestroika would be a good thing for the GDR as well. Then Wolf asks what glasnost and perestroika would be like in the family. The old conflicts rise up again. Wolf says that what Gorbachev wants to introduce in Moscow is something that he himself had demanded twenty years ago. And Gerhard had seen him as the enemy. In the end they sit facing one another in silence again. There seems to be no common way.

But Anne can't free herself from her father now either. Her relation with him is like a rope that connects her to her old life, that stops her being quite herself. Gerhard is the last remaining scrap of her dependence, and she herself will later say that it was only the downfall of the GDR that finally freed her from her childhood. On the other hand a different rope pulls her a few months later. She leaves the Party. The letter that she wrote to her Party group leader is in one of her files, wrapped in clear plastic like an important document. She writes: "I can no longer bear this attitude of denying reality that our leaders are assuming. The repression of reality has led to a paralysis of social life. A state of affairs like that is not just regrettable but also dangerous. Remaining in this completely ossified organization, which has long ceased to give signs of life, strikes me as pointless."

More and more people are disappearing to the West. That's how I get my first flat, which belonged to a girlfriend, a dancer in the Komische Oper, who didn't come back from a guest performance in West Berlin. In the summer the West German embassies in Budapest, Prague and Warsaw fill with refugees. At the same time something happens in the GDR. A force comes into being, unnoticeable at first, but growing with every passing week. It's like a big wave building up slowly and dragging along everything that isn't firmly anchored down. There isn't much to see on the surface, but there's a powerful pull in the depths. I remember an evening in August 1989 in the Church of the Redeemer in Lichtenberg, where I went with Anne. There are people there who call themselves civil-rights campaigners. They have strange haircuts and beards and a language that makes a strong impression on me because it's so honest and true. They say clearly and publicly what motivates them. That's completely new to me. I'm used to hearing something in skilful references, half-sentences, nuances, sensing hidden messages. It's often like that in the theatre. A little sentence, a key word, can inspire the audience because they themselves have finished the thought that had just been started, completed it silently in their heads and then shouting it out in delight. That art of hidden criticism, of disguised defiance, no longer seems to be necessary. The civil-rights campaigners in the Church of the Redeemer say the important thing now is to fight for fundamental freedoms, not to let ourselves be treated like children any more. The time for begging and pleading was over, now it was up to us as confident citizens to demand our rights.

I'm expecting something to happen, for people to be arrested on the spot or just forbidden to speak. But nothing happens. The people in the church clap and cheer. They call out "that's exactly right" and "let's do that right now". It's as if the prohibitions and the leaden anxiety had suddenly disappeared. Anne's just as surprised by this new tone, by the courage and the power in that church. Suddenly it's clear to me that it's much more exciting to stay here than go to Budapest or Prague to get over the border. The wave has caught me, it's pulling me along. A few days later I'm in the Gethsemane Church in Prenzlauer Berg. The people there are confident and cheerful too, in fact they're practically ecstatic. They all seem to have understood that something's happening, that it isn't just far away that national borders are coming down; our own borders are being marked out as well. I see a man standing in the street in front of the church, shouting at the top of his voice, as if he's just discovered the power of speech, as if he's incredibly happy just sensing who he is. Policemen are standing not far from the church. Minibuses are parked in the streets. Stasi men are walking around in front of the church, wanting to be recognized. They're showing us they're there, but they're hanging back.

Every time I come out of a church or a meeting I feel full of energy. In fact they always say and demand the same things. But it's always new, too. Like a rush that doesn't pass. You have to go to another meeting straight away to feel that rush. It's enough for you to look at each other, smile at each other on the U-Bahn, to know that you're both thinking exactly the same thing. There's a strange atmosphere in the city, excitement of the kind you get before going off on a big trip. I have the feeling that nothing can actually happen to us, not if there are so many of us. But that isn't so clear at this juncture.

In Peking demonstrators had been fired on in Tiananmen Square. The "Chinese solution" flickers through our heads as a possible scenario. We don't know how the GDR government will react. Whether it will swim away from the movement or try to break the wave by force.

Maxim after a visit to the Church of the Redeemer, 1989

In September 1989 there's a woman outside the door in Karlshorst. She's collecting signatures for the "New Forum". Anne signs and takes a few forms so that she can collect signatures as well. She meets up with friends and acquaintances in the Café Espresso on Unter den Linden. The list of signatures lies open on the table. She isn't scared now, even though the "New Forum" is still banned, even though no one knows what a signature like that might mean in the end. On 6 October 1989 Anne goes to her first meeting of opposition groups in the Church of the Redeemer. Television channels from all over the world are there to document the uprising. The groups present their programmes. A woman says they need to have free elections in the GDR under the supervision of the United Nations. Anne thinks that's taking it a bit far. Free elections. It would be enough for her if the Party listened to everybody from time to time. After the end of the event a call goes out for someone who speaks French, because a Belgian radio journalist wants an interview. Anne puts her hand up, thinking she's just going to have to translate. But it turns out that she's to give the interview herself. She's confused, she's worried about putting her foot in her mouth, but it's too late to back down. The journalist asks if she feels like an enemy of the GDR. Anne says the country's enemies are in the government and the Politburo. She's surprised and taken aback by her own words, it's as if she's on a flying carpet. She feels strong and happy.

Wolf goes to Leipzig with a few friends to paint a stage for a punk concert. The stage is in a derelict district in Leipzig East. He sees the dead chasms of houses, the deserted streets. In the evening, when the concert begins, the crumbling facades glow in the harsh stage lighting. They feel as if they're in a ghost town. In a café on the Ring, a drunken waiter insults the guests in a French-sounding fantasy language. A group from the West is alarmed. Wolf tells them not to take everything so seriously, because it will all soon be over. The Westerners don't understand what he means. They're hungry.

Anne and some others found the "New Forum" in Karlshorst. At the first meeting she's elected chairwoman. Journalists and historians from the West come to Anne and Wolf's flat every day. They sit in the kitchen, drink coffee, smoke and talk. In these conversations the old GDR has already ceased to exist. Instead another country has come into being, a democracy with different parties, but without private ownership, because this time everything really is to belong to the people. They talk about the Third Way, a compromise between capitalism and Socialism. Everything seems to be possible during these days, as long as the people are allowed to get on with it.

Wolf works tirelessly. He has so many ideas and so little time. He paints revolutionary banners for the Volksbühne and fabric pictures for a protest evening in the Church of the Redeemer. At night he sticks up posters in Alexanderplatz, calling for solidarity with Romania. He says he set off in the morning and had no idea what was happening. They days raced past him. There are two prints that must also have been produced at this time. Two figures, one turned in on itself and shivering, the other with broad shoulders and its head raised. Wolf calls these works "Fear" and "Pride". They are two souls that now live within him.

23

Speaking Choirs

I SEE THE PICTURES of the Monday demonstrations in Leipzig on television. Compared with these, things in Berlin are still quite quiet. There's a rumour that the first big Berlin demonstrations are going to be held on 7 October, the fortieth anniversary of the GDR. Rendezvous is at five o'clock by the World Time Clock on Alexanderplatz. On 3 October I have an appointment at police headquarters in Lichtenberg to pick up my visa for Hungary, which I applied for a month before. I'm amazed that visas are even being issued now, because the Hungarian Prime Minister has opened the border with Austria in the meantime, and any GDR citizen who is able to get as far as Hungary can emigrate without any difficulties. This little greenish form, written in German and Russian, could get me to the West. But I only want to leave if things go all Chinese in Berlin on 7 October. Somehow it's clear that this day will be crucial.

I'm already excited on the morning of 7 October. They're saying on the radio that Gorbachev and the leaders of the other Socialist states have already arrived in Berlin. The area around Alexanderplatz is guarded by police. Will we even get through to the World Time Clock? And how will they react if we disturb their birthday party? In the afternoon I go to Alexanderplatz with my girlfriend Christine. It's half past four and the only people to be seen are a few demonstrators and lots of police. I'm disappointed and wonder why the protest in Berlin isn't working. The people of Leipzig showed us how to do it. We get closer to the World Time Clock, and only now do I see that the whole of Alexanderplatz is full of people just waiting for things to kick off. Shortly after five the procession gets going, and at that moment people come streaming in from all directions. Soon the procession is too big to see all at once. We walk along Rathausstrasse to the Palace of the Republic. It's a good feeling, suddenly being with so many people. The fear has gone. Who's going to stop us now?

At the Palace of the Republic there's a wall of police trucks. Big grilles are mounted on the fronts of the trucks, clearly with a view to pushing the demonstrators aside. In the Palace, Erich Honecker is welcoming the heads of state of the brother countries. We shout "Gorbi, Gorbi", because we want to see Gorbachev. But there's no sign of him. Instead the police try to force us away. The trucks get moving and push the crowds back. Stasi men fish out individual demonstrators and lead them away. There's a feeling of unease, and no one really seems to know where it goes from here. Someone has a megaphone and shouts that we're now marching to Prenzlauer Berg. The procession reforms and pushes its way up Karl Liebknecht Strasse. Stasi people, police and FDJ members try to stop us. They link arms and block the street, but they're overrun. I see a young woman in an FDJ shirt, standing distraught, crying in the street. She bellows, "Why are you doing that?"

Right beside us two Stasi try to drag a man away. Three demonstrators leap in and start hitting the Stasi men. One of them falls backwards and lies in the street, the other thinks for a moment and runs away. I can still see the fleeing Stasi man in front of my eyes. The horror in his eyes. How dare these people defend themselves!

The police at the side of the street look on but do nothing. "They're scared," shouts one of the demonstrators. "The cops are shitting themselves."

The further we walk, the more powerful we feel. The speaking choirs ring out in the empty streets. People come running out of the houses and join us, others wave at us from their windows. The mood is relaxed now, the tension and fear have fled. We walk to the Gethsemane Church, where the procession breaks up. A few hundred demonstrators sit down in the road, candles are lit, songs are sung. The police trucks with the grilles approach from all sides. A policeman shouts through a megaphone that this is an illegal riotous assembly, and anyone who doesn't leave immediately will be arrested. Suddenly the fear is back. My friend Christine and I wonder what we're doing. We don't want to be arrested. What good would that do? The demonstrations were a success, and there will be other demonstrations. We leave. With a bad conscience, because we're leaving the people with the candles alone. The people who are braver than us.

Christine lives on Anklamer Strasse, right near the Wall. We walk down Eberswalder Strasse and see that hundreds of soldiers are standing side by side in front of the Wall. They stand there in silence, lit only by the street lamps, sub-machine guns on their backs, hands folded in front of them, staring straight ahead. They're standing all the way down the street. It's only then that I realize how threatened the state feels. And how it's misjudged the demonstrators. Because this evening it wouldn't have occurred to anybody to storm the wall, when the important thing right now is to change the things inside it. An officer checks our IDs to see if we really need to go along here to get home. We walk along the silent row of men, hear our footsteps on the damp cobbles. A moment ago we passed through Berlin, singing and cheering. A moment ago the street still belonged to us. Now we're orderly citizens again, saying thank you nicely to the officers, glad to be allowed home.

The next day everything is terribly normal again. On the stairs I meet our neighbour, who is on her way home from the shops and wasn't even aware of our demonstration. In the street where the Wall stands, the soldiers have moved away again, and children are French-skipping on the pavement. Life goes on, as if nothing has happened. On the East German news, the demonstration isn't mentioned, but there are pictures of the night on Western television. They show policemen tearing into the demonstrators, and a young woman, bloody but smiling, talking about a victory. In the afternoon I go with Christine to visit a friend of my parents. Anne and Wolf are there too, and we tell them about our night. It already seems a very long time ago. Anne is concerned, and tells us to be careful because the state is capable of anything right now. She's seen the policemen clubbing demonstrators on television. But I think she's also a bit proud of us. Wolf is cross because he didn't know anything about the demonstration. He wishes he'd been there. Anne says it would have been too hot for her. Demonstrating against the state, on the Republic's birthday. It would have been like a provocation. "Exactly," says Wolf and shakes his head.

My parents' friend gives us a copy of an illegal church newspaper, in which she describes why she's just left the Party. Christine puts the newspaper in her pocket because I haven't got one. On the way home we're planning to take the U-Bahn at Alexanderplatz station. On the platform a man in plain clothes comes up to us, and there's another one standing behind us. The man wants to see our IDs, I ask why but get no answer. The IDs disappear and the man tells us to come with them. I see other people being led away along the platform. Perhaps they don't want us to take the line towards the

Wolf, 1989

Gethsemane Church, I think. The man pushes us abruptly towards the U-Bahn exit. We walk up the stairs and see police trucks waiting in Alexanderplatz. We're searched, and I remember the church newspaper that Christine has in her coat pocket. I'm about to whisper something to her, but it's too late. A policeman is holding the paper in his hand and asking where we got it. "Found it in the S-Bahn," says Christine. She is led away, and I have to get into one of the trucks. There are already about twenty young people sitting on benches in the back. It all seems like a bad dream to me. I can't get my head round it, we've been arrested and still haven't even done anything.

The trucks set off, I ask two boys sitting next to me what's actually going on. But they don't know any more than I do. They say they'd been at the cinema and had just been taken away. A girl cries and asks if we're all going to jail. I can't stop thinking about Christine and the newspaper. I can't see where we're going, because the roof of the truck is covered over. Cold air blows through the gaps in the tarpaulin, there's a smell of diesel and sweat. The truck stops after about half an hour. The tarpaulins are thrown back, and a policeman shouts at us to get out and stand with our hands behind our heads. We're standing in a courtyard, there's barbed wire stretched along the tops of the walls. Are we already in jail? There are about thirty armed policemen standing around us. One of them, a small, thin man with black leather boots, yells that we all know why we're there. He calls us a "shower" and a "rabble" and threatens us with extremely harsh treatment if any of us even thinks of acting contrary to his orders. We're to line up in three rows in a big, brightly lit garage, "one metre's distance from the man in front and behind, eyes front and keep your traps shut".

We stand in the garage all night. I spend hours looking at the shoulders of the man in front of me, because looking at the floor isn't allowed. The man in front of me has brown hair and wears a dark-blue jacket. Even today I don't know what his face looks like. I wonder what's going to happen to us, what accusations they can actually bring against us. If it wasn't for the church newspaper, I wouldn't actually need to worry. The longer I think, the more anxious I become. Perhaps we'll disappear into jail for weeks or months, without contact with the outside world. The government has nothing more to lose anyway, and after the demonstration on 7 October they may have opted for the harsh, Chinese-style response. What's a dictatorship capable of when it feels it's been cornered? I start imagining the most terrible scenarios. I always do that when I'm scared. Maybe to be able to tell myself it's not going to be as bad as that. And then I think of Gerhard, and that he's bound to come and get me out of here if necessary. If Gerhard could see me here, his grandson, innocently arrested. Would he still defend the state, or would he be ashamed? He'd help me at any rate. The thought reassures me a little.

Eventually someone in the garage just sits down. He says he can't stand up any more. Two policemen pull him up from the floor and lead him away, no idea where. At dawn I ask a policeman to take me to the toilet. On the way I look around. It looks as if we've ended up in a police barracks. But it's not a prison, at least. I tell the policeman that none of us actually know why we're here. "We'll see," says the policeman and brings me back to my place in the garage. A few hours later the first of us are taken to the main building "for interrogation". When my name is called I'm almost relieved that this damned waiting is over. I'm taken to a room with a desk and a picture of Honecker hanging over it. Honecker smiles, but the man behind the desk just growls at me to sit down. He's quite old, with grey hair and a bald patch. He doesn't look angry, more as if the whole business is starting to get on his nerves. "The sooner you tell the truth, the better it'll be for you," he says. The man wants to know what I did the evening before I was arrested. I tell him about meeting my parents' friend and say we just wanted to go home. The man asks where the church newspaper came from, the one he found on Christine. I tell him we found it in the S-Bahn, as Christine said. The man shouts at me not to treat him like an idiot. "Your friend has admitted everything, so don't act stupid." I notice my hand starting to shake, my face glows red. "OK, out with it," says the man. I don't know what to do. It's possible that Christine hasn't admitted anything at all, that he's just trying to trick me. But I feel the urge just to tell him everything, because then at least it will all be over. The man offers me a cigarette and suddenly it all comes spilling out. I tell him we got the paper from my parents' friend, that Christine has nothing to do with it. That's the end of the interrogation, and I'm taken to a waiting room. It's only now that I realize I'm completely drenched in sweat. I feel miserable. I would have loved to be brave, but I couldn't. I'm a failure, a wimp.

Two hours later I'm allowed to go. I call my parents from a phone box. Anne tells me to come home quickly, Christine's there already. I go to Karlshorst and walk along the street from the station to our house. Everything's quiet, there are just a few crows cawing above the railway embankment. I feel as if I've been away for ever. Before I tell them about my night, Anne fetches a tape recorder. She says everything needs to be documented. She's being more of a historian than a mother; maybe that makes it easier for her. When I started writing this book, Anne gave me the cassette she made. It's interesting to hear my voice again after such a long time. I speak quietly and in a very detached way, as if it wasn't my story. I think it was very embarrassing for me to be a victim. They hit me where it hurt, they injured my sense of self. I don't mention the flyers, my anxiety, my defeat. I had a guilty conscience about it for ages afterwards. That interrogation remained a dark chapter. Later I ran through it in my memory over and over again, giving the answers I would actually have expected of myself. I did the same with the discussions in citizenship class. I was disappointed with myself, and it was much worse than the night in the garage.

Christine told me later that her father had worked for the Stasi. She said she'd been more afraid of him that night than she had been of the police. And still she was braver than I was. Much later we found out that the friend of my parents who gave us the church newspaper had also worked for the Stasi. It's hard to grasp, hard to tease out good from bad.

It's all forgotten for the time being in the events that follow daily. All of a sudden people are willing to take risks. There are spontaneous demos, parties and trade unions are founded, appeals are made, signatures collected. The whole country is turned upside down. People are talking, openly and freely, for the first time. I remember one evening in the House of the Teacher on Alexanderplatz. Hundreds of teachers, pupils and parents sat together, discussing what had actually happened in the schools during all those years. They talked about the lies, about constraints, about the game we played with ourselves. A history teacher stands up and says tearfully that she wants to apologize to everyone she's wronged. Then she collapses and has to be tended to by an emergency doctor. In the Deutsches Theater the actors line up on the stage and call in chorus for courage and change. In Bebelplatz SED propagandists are whistled down. The wave that has been building up over weeks and months breaks through all the dams, shoves fear and caution aside and swirls up the alluvial past from the depths. There is no certainty now, and no truth, our cherished beliefs and sacred tenets are crumbling to the ground. There isn't even a big bang, everything is just silently dissolving, even the things we thought were made of concrete. It all happens so quickly that no one can really cope with the astonishment and the comprehension. Forty years are washed away within only a few days. And every time you think you've reached solid ground the next abyss opens up.

Even today I'm impressed by the speed with which people became aware of their power and dignity, how alert their instincts were, how great their hunger for freedom and truth. Those great words had suddenly regained their meaning. You just had to look round to understand that. There was this pride in the eyes of the men and women who sat at the round tables and negotiated the future with the representatives of the bankrupt state, there was the bright voice of the fourteen-year-old girl who stood in the Church of the Redeemer and told about how she had distributed handwritten flyers with her little sister, there were the tears of the women who were released from the Stasi prison in Hohenschönhausen, and there was that dead look on Erich Honecker's face when he was voted out of the Politburo.

On the evening of 9 November I watch the programme *Tagesthemen* with Christine, and the presenter Hajo Friedrichs says the gates of the Berlin Wall are wide open. We quickly get dressed and go down to the street, where there are other people who have also just been watching *Tagesthemen*. A man drives us to the border crossing at Heinrich Heine Strasse. There are a few hundred people standing by the barrier at the departure hall. The border guards say they haven't heard anything about the Wall being opened. Then a policeman comes along and says we should go to the "House of Travel" on Alexanderplatz, because exit papers are being issued there. The people run off and jump in their cars. We travel with a married couple. The man's hands are shaking with excitement, and I'm worried that he's going to have an accident and we'll miss the opening of the Wall. The "House of Travel" is locked and in darkness. It's only now that we understand that the policeman was probably just trying to gain some time. How could we be so silly as to think that you would need exit papers in a situation like this?

We drive to Checkpoint Charlie, and even from a distance it's clear that the Wall is now open. People are cheering and shouting. A woman stands weeping beside us. She says she was twenty when the border was built. "Then it was just there, and now it's just gone like that and my life is probably just over like that." She weeps with fury and joy, and I wish I could weep too. But as always in situations like this, when I feel that one should really be overwhelmed, I can't do it. All the emotions bounce off me, they don't get to me. I stand there and look at everything as if I'm not even a part of it. Christine is the same, we hold hands, allow ourselves to be pushed towards the open gate and are incapable of saying anything. The border guards don't even want to see our passports, they wave us through, we walk past the guards' shacks, see the brightly lit death strip, and perhaps twenty metres away the Wall, where people sit waving. We cross the white line separating East from West. A man tries to hug me, but that's too much for me. I have the feeling that my brain's too slow to grasp it all. It's like a film playing out in front of me. Christine cries, we hug, and I need a cigarette.

That evening on *Tagesschau* Anne and Wolf see Politburo member Günter Schabowski reading out a declaration. It's about a new regulation for travel to the West. Anne, practised in understanding

Politburo announcements, grasps that it's about GDR citizens who want to leave the country. Wolf suggests going to the Wall, but Anne is tired, and she doesn't want to go to the West anyway. "What's going to be going on at the Wall anyway?" she says, and Wolf allows himself to be persuaded to stay at home. At half past ten they go to bed. And when they wake up the next morning, the GDR has already almost disappeared.

EPILOGUE

T HE MONDAY AFTER THE FALL of the Wall I went to a police
station in Kreuzberg and applied for a Western passport. It
was a precautionary measure. I wanted to have something in my
hand just in case the Wall closed again. I presented my GDR identity card, and the officer in the police station got up from his chair,
shook my hand and said he was glad that I was finally free as well.
He called in a few colleagues, and they beamed too and shook my
hand. It was embarrassing, I felt like a Bushman being greeted by
white men in civilization. The passport would be sorted out straight
away, because I was basically a West German by birth, and because
of adverse circumstances it was only now that I was able to collect
my passport. By adverse circumstances he meant the GDR. Half
an hour later I was holding my passport, which was green and said
in gold letters that I was now a real Westerner.

A few weeks later I went to the East with my Western passport.
That was a strange business, because I'd always dreamt of it, and now
everything was different. The GDR was only apparently there, and
any Easterner could now be a Westerner as well. There was also the
fact that Westerners were starting to get on my nerves. They talked
about the GDR as if it were a cholera zone. They said we'd been
corrupted by dictatorship, that we had weak characters and were
badly educated. I took that personally, which made me additionally

insecure, because I actually didn't want to have anything to do with the GDR. But suddenly there it was, this feeling that I hadn't known before. This "we" that I'd found it so hard to say. I think I never felt so close to the GDR as I did after its downfall.

For the initial period after the fall of the Wall Anne would ideally have liked to stay at home. She would have sat in her armchair on the veranda with a pot of tea and a book. As if nothing had happened, as if the world out there were just as unchanged as her comfortable study. But that wasn't going to happen, she had to get out because my little brother was desperate to see the West. Wolf had backache and went to bed for a few days. So on the first weekend after the fall of the Wall Anne crossed the Oberbaum Bridge with my brother. They could hardly move, because the whole of the GDR seemed to be in West Berlin. An endless procession of people drifted through the streets, it was impossible to escape the crowds. Anne says it was one of the most terrible days of her life. She saw all those people, all those happy faces, and she sensed that something was coming to an end even though it hadn't yet really got going. The reforms, the Third Way, it was all just a dream. After a few hundred metres into the West she noticed that she couldn't speak. All that came out of her throat was a quiet croaking sound. It had left her speechless.

Anne says she was worried at the time that the whole of her life's meaning would disappear with the GDR. She couldn't imagine being without this country, which had always been there. She felt as if she were on a revolving stage that turns around and suddenly creates a new world where the old one was a moment before. It all went so quickly. But then she was amazed that she wasn't actually sad. That she didn't even need to cry. It was more as if a burden had fallen from her. She no longer needed the GDR, that unhappy love of her youth. She had grown up.

When she got her voice back, Anne became the spokeswoman for the "New Forum" in the district of Lichtenberg, and later the press spokeswoman for the faction Alliance '90/The Greens in the East Berlin City Council Assembly. She found that interesting for a while, but then she wanted to stop talking for other people and start talking for herself at last. She didn't know exactly what would happen next, but she enjoyed the openness, the new possibilities. She'd had enough of certainties. She got out the essays she'd written in the last years of the GDR. The essays became books and Anne became a noted historian. She dissected the country she had loved, and which had caused her such pain. She looked at it with the cool gaze of the academic. That gaze created distance, it made it easier for her to say goodbye. The GDR had become history for her.

Wolf couldn't enjoy the new freedom, it drove him up the wall. He couldn't sleep, night after night, worrying about the future. His employers were liquidated, a policeman from Bielefeld who had inherited the house in Karlshorst wanted to throw them out of the flat, a community of heirs from West Berlin demanded the cottage in Basdorf back. When he lay awake at night, he saw himself living under a bridge, a homeless artist, a failure from the East. He missed the security that he had previously found so constricting. He missed the friction he got from rubbing up against the state. The West offered no edges, no resistance. He could do what he wanted now, there was no answer, no reaction. The new country was like a block of foam rubber, you could thump it, but it left no impression. Who was he supposed to make art for now? And above all, against whom?

Post-Wall, his paintings become sadder and sadder, his figures kneel with their heads lowered. Or just lie there, bare-chested, under circling crows, the Brandenburg Gate casting long shadows in the distance. "Opening the Wall" is the caption to the drawing. He wrote a short text for an installation that was shown on Church Day in Potsdam in 1993: "Faith in progress is shattered, the literal future, the question of the rate of growth in association with the meaning of life and ecological disasters is producing a Titanic mentality. The fight for a place in the lifeboat is on. Fear of cold water."

He launched a project with Nil, his painter friend from Savignyplatz. In autumn 1990 a small black sign hung on the door of the Charlottenburg gallery. "Nil-West, Leo-East", it said. It was an experiment. They both wanted to show that Easterners and Westerners could get something moving together. But it went bank-rupt, because nothing moved at all. Wolf wanted to let something grow slowly and talk a lot. Nil wanted to run off straight away and stir up the whole art market. Wolf accused Nil of only being after money. Nil accused Wolf of being too quiet and circumspect. The two men who wanted to be avant-gardists froze into a cliché of East and West. After a few months Nil took the black sign down from the gallery door. It was over. And Wolf was disappointed by the West, just as he had previously been disappointed by the GDR. He wanted to do something new, just get running. But his creativity drowned in worries. He worked on job-creation projects, took courses paid for by the employment exchange. He was like a wolf from the zoo who suddenly has to cope in the wild. The zoo was shut.

*

Werner, 1985

Werner went on living the way he'd always lived. He spent the summer in a cabin that he'd built in 1970 in the grounds of the Sports Association on Lake Zeesen. A simple wooden cabin, four metres by four, without water or electricity. "My paradise," Werner had written under a colour drawing that he made in 1992. He's sitting outside the cabin at a laid table in the warm evening light. A woman is coming out of the door carrying a tray and smiling at him. The drawing hangs in his bedroom in Berlin, beside the portrait of his daughter Karola and a photograph of Hildegard, his second, late wife.

Werner used to lie on the banks of Lake Zeesen with Grandma Sigrid when they met in the late Twenties. They swam there and played fistball with the others. Werner sometimes looked at the smooth, sparkling water. And he wished everything would stay like that for ever. At least that's how he describes it in a poem about the lake, written "during a sleepless night in December 1989". The poem ends with the lines, "You handsome, sole, true friend, we have never lost one another. Whatever else may happen, you are my lucky charm."

I don't know why Werner couldn't sleep on that night in December 1989. Whether he was thinking about his life. Or whether he was worried about the future. That poem about Lake Zeesen sounds like the assessment of a man who has understood at the end of his life how futile everything was. The second verse says: "All the things I believed, and afterwards was stripped of all hope. But you, old man, never let me down, you were there when I needed you, you never fled."

Werner died on 30 December 2008. It's strange that this grandfather, whom I'd only just discovered, is gone for ever. I was at the funeral, I threw sand on his urn and felt nothing. A cemetery musician played 'The Song of the Little Trumpeter'. I learnt the song in school. It ends with the words: "Sleep well, little trumpeter, merry blood of the Red Guard."

Gerhard now has a French speech therapist, because he understands French words better than German ones since he had his stroke. The doctors say Gerhard's brain can only respond to words that are connected with an important emotional experience. Perhaps France really did become his home at some stage. At least the country was his vanishing point when the GDR was over, when his language was still there but he no longer knew what he was supposed to say. He travelled around France giving readings for weeks at a time. The book about his time in the Resistance had just been published in French, and he probably preferred talking about that time than about what was happening at home. German unity was a bugbear for Gerhard.

All of a sudden it was back, the Greater Germany. And his little anti-fascist GDR was lost for ever. He once told me how much he liked the fact that the French saw everything with the same sceptical eye as he did. In France he felt freed from his fears, his disappointment.

In the years that followed I think the GDR slowly faded from his thoughts. When I asked him about it, it was as if he had to spend a long time looking for it. Once, as a joke, I wished him a Happy Birthday of the Republic on 7 October, and he had no idea what I was talking about. He even lost the names of important comrades, people he had known himself. Instead he retreated more and more into his youth, his days with the partisans. He went to schools again and talked about his struggle against the fascists, he appeared as an eyewitness at rallies and conferences. Again and again he travelled around the sites of his struggle, accompanied by camera crews. It was as if his whole life had shrunk to the few years that had probably always been the most important for him.

I recently visited him in Friedrichshagen. His French speech therapist was there, and he was learning words just as he had done in the children's hospital in Paris. He was very alert and concentrated, and sometimes he laughed. Perhaps he was remembering the beautiful doctor, his first love. That woman who had made him a Frenchman.

I often visit Basdorf now, the little house with the big garden. A few years ago I drove by to see what became of my childhood paradise. The garden was completely overgrown, but the house looked the same as ever. I called one of the heirs from West Berlin who got the property back after the fall of the Wall, because it had belonged to them before the Wall was built. The man said on the phone that he didn't know what to do with the shack. He meant our house. I asked him if he would lease the property to me, and two weeks later I had the key. I opened the door, and there on the veranda was the table that Wolf had built when I was four. The checked curtains still hung in the nursery. Even the smell was the same.

Now, at the weekends, we often cycle along the road that runs through the beech wood to Lake Liepnitz. There are no big animals there now, the wall and the signs have gone. You can visit the houses in the forest where the members of the Politburo once lived. They are simple houses with grey facades. On the peninsula in Lake Liepnitz, where Erich Honecker had his swimming spot, there's now a field for sunbathing. We play there with the children in the sun, jump off the jetty into the water, where the soldiers once stood with their sub-machine guns. Now and again I tell the children what it was like back then, and they tell me I've told them that hundreds of times. Then I feel as if I've prematurely aged. As if my life is already behind me.

Those weekends in Basdorf are lovely, but they're confusing, too. Everything in this country has changed, but the house, the table in the veranda and the checked curtains remain. It's like a museum of childhood, like a piece of the GDR that has outlived everything. Even the birch tree behind the house, the one I used to climb, hasn't changed. Perhaps it's because we've both grown.

PUSHKIN PRESS

Pushkin Press was founded in 1997. Having first rediscovered European classics of the twentieth century, Pushkin now publishes novels, essays, memoirs, children's books, and everything from timeless classics to the urgent and contemporary.

Pushkin books like this one represent exciting, high-quality writing from around the world. Pushkin publishes widely acclaimed, brilliant authors such as Stefan Zweig, Marcel Aymé, Antal Szerb, Paul Morand and Yasushi Inoue, as well as some of the most exciting contemporary and often prize-winning writers, including Andrés Neuman, Edith Pearlman and Ryu Murakami.

Pushkin Press publishes the world's best stories, to be read and read again.

*

Pushkin Press

Pushkin Press was founded in 1997, and publishes novels, essays, memoirs, children's books—everything from timeless classics to the urgent and contemporary. Our books represent exciting, high-quality writing from around the world: we publish some of the twentieth century's most widely acclaimed, brilliant authors such as Stefan Zweig, Marcel Aymé, Antal Szerb, Gaito Gazdanov and Yasushi Inoue, as well as compelling and award-winning contemporary writers, including Andrés Neuman, Edith Pearlman, Erwin Mortier and Ayelet Gundar-Goshen.

Pushkin Press publishes the world's best stories, to be read and read again. Here are just some of the titles from our long and varied list. For more amazing stories, visit www.pushkinpress.com.

═══

THE SPECTRE OF ALEXANDER WOLF

GAITO GAZDANOV

'A mesmerising work of literature' Antony Beevor

BINOCULAR VISION

EDITH PEARLMAN

'A genius of the short story' Mark Lawson, *Guardian*

IN THE BEGINNING WAS THE SEA

TOMÁS GONZÁLEZ

'Smoothly intriguing narrative, with its touches of sinister, Patricia Highsmith-like menace' *Irish Times*

BEWARE OF PITY

STEFAN ZWEIG

'Zweig's fictional masterpiece' *Guardian*